How to Write an Exceptional Thesis or Dissertation

A Step-By-Step Guide from Proposal to Successful Defense

By J.S. Graustein

How to Write an Exceptional Thesis or Dissertation:
A Step-By-Step Guide from Proposal to Successful Defense

Copyright © 2014 by Atlantic Publishing Group, Inc.
1405 SW 6th Ave. • Ocala, Florida 34471 • 352-622-1825 • 352-622-1875–Fax
Website: www.atlantic-pub.com • E-mail: sales@atlantic-pub.com
SAN Number: 268-1250

Library of Congress Cataloging-in-Publication Data

Graustein, J.S.
  How to write an exceptional thesis or dissertation : a step-by-step guide from proposal to successful defense / by J.S. Graustein.
      p. cm.
  Includes bibliographical references and index.
  ISBN-13: 978-1-60138-603-8 (alk. paper)
  ISBN-10: 1-60138-603-6 (alk. paper)
  1. Dissertations, Academic--Research--Methodology. 2. Academic writing. I. Title.
  LB2369.G695 2010
  001.4'2--dc22
                                2010032488

BOOK PRODUCTION DESIGN: T.L. Price • tlpricefreelance@gmail.com
FRONT AND BACK COVER DESIGN: Jackie Miller • millerjackiej@gmail.com

Printed on Recycled Paper

Printed in the United States

Over the years, we have adopted a number of dogs from rescues and shelters. First there was Bear and after he passed, Ginger and Scout. Now, we have Kira, another rescue. They have brought immense joy and love not just into our lives, but into the lives of all who met them.

We want you to know a portion of the profits of this book will be donated in Bear, Ginger and Scout's memory to local animal shelters, parks, conservation organizations, and other individuals and nonprofit organizations in need of assistance.

– Douglas & Sherri Brown,
President & Vice-President of Atlantic Publishing

Acknowledgements:

I would never have started writing this book if it were not for my experience as a graduate student of the Department of Biological Sciences at Northern Illinois University. I sincerely thank all the faculty and graduate students from 1992 to 1995 for teaching me how to think and learn, especially the crew that showed me the recuperative power of pool at the Box Office and music by Howard and the White Boys. I would also like to thank the undergraduate students from the same time period, those who assisted me with data-collection and those who allowed me to experiment on them while I learned how to teach. To my adviser, Dr. Carl N. von Ende and my teaching model, Dr. Bethia King, I give special thanks for encouraging me to develop the communicative, organizational, and interpersonal skills that were the eventual basis of my ability to finish writing this book.

Dedication:

To Kurt, for giving me a chair, and Mel, for keeping me in it.

Table of Contents

Chapter 2: Explore   63

Chapter 3: Read   83

Chapter 4: Design　　　　　　　　　99

Chapter 5: Propose   135

Chapter 6: Test   173

Chapter 7: Analyze   189

Chapter 8: Write   211

Chapter 9: Defend   235

Chapter 10: Share   257

Introduction

Presumably, you picked up this book because you have finished the majority of your graduate coursework and are ready to begin working on your thesis or dissertation, but you are not sure how to go about it. You might also be looking for a way to avoid being another "unfinished" statistic.

You are certainly not alone. According to the National Center for Education, approximately 756,000 students earn a master's degree per year and 175,000 students earn their doctoral degree. In the same year, 63,712 students earned their doctoral degree. It is easy for students to not finish their graduate work because of the amount of work involved. But, with the right approach, finishing a graduate degree will become less complicated.

RATIONALE FOR THIS BOOK

So, how long have you worked toward your degree? How much has changed in your life since you began your journey? Life does not pause just because you are in graduate school. Many students take longer than the typical graduate catalog advises. Taking longer to complete the curriculum can create a frustration.

This book is designed to alleviate that frustration by:

- Keeping you focused and productive no matter what life throws at you during the thesis/dissertation process.

- Preventing wasted time so your actual time spent earning your degree is as close to your initial expectations as possible.

- Helping you build a network that will maximize your potential as a student and professional.

- Realigning your vision of what a thesis/dissertation is and what you need/want to accomplish from it.

- Taking the mystery out of the thesis/dissertation process and demonstrating you can finish.

MY PERSONAL EXPERIENCE

I received my Master of Science degree in 1995 from the Department of Biological Sciences at Northern Illinois University. Enrolled full time, I took nine semesters to finish a six-semester program. Considering I was on academic probation after my first semester, it was a miracle I finished at all.

What happened, you ask? I landed on campus with zero idea of what it meant to be a graduate student. My first semester of coursework quickly demonstrated classroom expectations. But, that coursework did not teach me how to read and use academic papers. Thanks to the graduate school catalog, I knew I needed an adviser for the thesis requirement, yet it took me three months of knocking on administrative and departmental doors to figure out advisers were not assigned; it was my job to find one.

When I enrolled, I had wanted to study algae. But because of faculty constraints and a one-month stint in a research lab, I switched to the more realistic topic of wetland plants. My long-suffering adviser, who specialized in aquatic insects, worked outside his comfort zone to help me develop a question of local significance. He also helped me acquire research locations and connections to local experts.

My fellow graduate students invited me to unofficial seminars where we read and discussed academic papers, thus teaching me one essential skill I lacked — the ability to analyze sources. One student in particular, who you will meet later in a Case Study, mentored me in organization and departmental politics. I also tagged along on various data-collection jaunts, helping doctorate candidates and myself at the same time. I never would have finished my degree without this peer network.

My thesis project involved growing wetland plants on a patch of land the university owned. I spent my first field season learning about the invasive grass and native sedge I was to study. This immediately banished any thought of finishing in six semesters. But, even the most knowledgeable and prepared person cannot prevent acts of God from interfering with timetables. My second field season was hampered by drought; I had to water my study subjects with a 5-gallon watering can to keep them alive. Unfortunately, I made the mistake of watering one experimental set from a pond filled with tadpoles and the other from a frog-free creek, essentially adding an unintentional water-quality variable to an already multivariate design. Fortunately, I remembered to record the event in my field notebook, as the protein-rich, live fertilizer could have impacted the growth of one batch. It certainly made for a funny story during my defense.

What should have been my third field season was preempted by flood and an impending move. Thanks to my creative committee, though, I had managed to conduct a greenhouse experiment the previous winter and spring that padded my miserable excuse for summer data so I could successfully defend and earn my degree anyway — two weeks before I was to relocate to California for my husband's new job. I successfully defended, made my revisions, filed my thesis, moved cross-country, and then flew back for the graduation ceremony. My adviser threw a party at his home to celebrate; brats and beer never tasted so good.

HOW TO USE THIS BOOK

As a graduate student, you have already read copious amounts of material, so adding a thick how-to book to your stack might seem like a big task. But, this book is designed to be read and followed chapter by chapter. It should serve as a guide as you complete the process of writing your dissertation or thesis. You will master concepts and working habits as you go, building on prior-chapter skills as you develop new ones.

Each chapter contains tasks associated with the core elements of a successful thesis/dissertation, elements that are interdependent and continuous throughout the process. These elements are:

- **Topic:** Everything from your broad interests to your specific research problem

- **Literature:** The vast and ever-expanding record of knowledge about your topic

- **Assistance:** The giving and receiving of help in a variety of contexts

- **Data:** The designing, collecting, and analyzing of information pertaining to your research problem

- **Written work:** Notes, outlines, proposal, and the main scholarly work

- **Organization:** Time management, scheduling, filing, and disaster recovery

Because this book by its nature must force a fairly nonlinear process into a linear framework, each chapter will end with a list of tasks from that chapter grouped by phases. Each phase within a chapter may or may not have tasks from every element. The nice thing about the grouping is it gives you choices when you are stuck in that "I should be doing something for my thesis right now, but I do not know what" mode. You will be more likely to get something done if you can choose from a list rather than bang away at the one item you do not feel like doing.

Chapter titles are written in the imperative to keep you focused while completing each stage of the research process. For instance, if you are in Chapter 8, but you find yourself spending five hours in the library doing literature searches at the level of Chapter 3, stop. Remind yourself it is time to write, not read. When you actually finish your degree, you will be glad you did.

Chapter 1: Prepare

This chapter will be like taking a massive breath before diving into the deep end of a pool. You will prepare yourself for the expectations, requirements, and functions of theses and dissertations. You will walk through the first steps of choosing a topic and accessing the academic literature for your future topic. And, because you presumably have never written a thesis/dissertation before, this chapter will help you find the wealth of assistance available from faculty, support services, and other graduate students. Statistical anxiety, lack of organization, and degree-threatening disaster can be conquered by a little preparation, laid out in this book.

TOPIC: CHOOSING A FOCUS

Choice of topic is the most important aspect of the thesis/dissertation process. Topic drives your choice of research problem, and your research problem drives everything else: the literature you read, the methodology you design, even the professional network you build. So although it may be possible to finish quickly using a ready-made topic within a professor's specialty, be sure it is in the vicinity of what you intend to pursue after graduation. This topic will be the foundation of your career; make sure it can support the house you want to live in.

From broad interest to main topic

To start your thinking process, take a look at your department's faculty directory on your university's website. Chances are each professor is listed by name and research specialty. They are all studying within the same discipline, but they have found niches for themselves where they can make a difference. Now it is your turn to find yourself a niche.

Areas of interest from your coursework

It takes nine to 15 hours of coursework to prepare for thesis research and more for dissertation research. You have already narrowed down your interest by selecting that coursework. What are the most fascinating things you learned during those courses?

- Jot the first ten that pop into your head on the nearest scrap of paper.
- Place a star next to any items you found supremely easy to understand.
- Place a star next to any items you found yourself thinking about long after class was over.
- Check your list against the research specialties of your department's faculty, and place a star next to any items that match.

With any luck, you found at least five matches, considering someone from the department probably taught the courses that piqued your interest. Check to see if there are any items that have multiple stars next to them. These could be some topics you might want to keep in mind for later.

Constraints

Interest and research speciality alone are not the only considerations when selecting a topic. Practical constraints must be taken under consideration. Narrow down the list from the previous section by taking the following actions:

- Place a star next to the matched items whose faculty are teaching full time rather than adjunct (associated with the university but not necessarily on a tenure track) or emeritus (retired but still retaining office space and/or a limited course load).

- Place a star next to any items from courses in which you got along with the professor.

- Place a star next to any items that have local significance.

- If travel is an issue for you, cross out any items that would require travel in order to collect data.

- If time is an issue for you, cross out any items that would require repeated data collection over the course of several years.

- If you found an item interesting yet difficult to understand, cross it out. The research process itself is fraught with frustration. These items would be better suited to post-degree research.

On a fresh sheet of paper, write down the three items with the most stars. If any are tied for third place, write down all the tied items. If the list has nothing but crossed out items, jot down a new list of ten fascinating things, and start over. Eventually, you will end up with a list of three potential topics. Be sure you are comfortable with all three before moving on.

Basic versus applied approaches

Think for a moment about why you chose to embark on your graduate degree journey. Was it for career advancement? Was it to solve a problem and make a difference in the world? Was it because you are intensely curious and never want to stop learning? Knowing your core reason for seeking a graduate degree will help you focus on which side of the research road you want to start: basic or applied.

Basic research is research for the sake of knowing something. It is sometimes referred to as pure research; it benefits the human race by exploring the whys and hows of life, thus feeding the need to understand the world.

Applied research, on the other hand, is research for the sake of discovering or improving something. Applied research is sometimes referred to as practical research; it benefits the human race by finding solutions to problems, thus making life easier to live.

For instance, lettuce varieties that show resistance to aphid attack would be studied with an applied approach. The popularity of backyard gardening throughout the last century would lend itself to a basic approach. Both research topics have the potential to involve lettuce and gardening. But, the aphid topic focuses on what can be done in the future to solve a problem, while the popularity topic focuses on what has happened in the past, why it might have happened that way, and what might happen in the future.

Which approach interests you more? If you entered graduate school for advancement opportunities or to make a difference, you will most likely be attracted to a topic that lends itself to applied questions. If you entered graduate school because of insatiable curiosity, you will most likely be drawn to a topic that serves to further your knowledge of your interests. However, either topic is legitimate as long as you will be happy and invested in the result.

Look over your top-three list from the previous section, and write applied or basic next to each item. If you see an item that could be researched using either approach, write "both" next to it. If you are strongly attracted to one approach, circle the items with that label. Hopefully, you have at least one topic circled. Regardless, move on to the next section. Please note you may wish to repeat the listing procedure as you learn more during the entire preparation stage.

LITERATURE: FINDING SOURCES OF POTENTIAL TOPICS

Whether the above listing process yielded any viable topics, surveying the local research landscape will prepare you for interactions with experts you may encounter during your thesis/dissertation journey. For the purpose of this discussion, the term "local experts" refers to anyone within easy driving distance who has experience in your discipline. Local experts can:

- Open doors for you in accessing data or study populations
- Alert you to snags you may find in the literature or topics about which you won't find much literature
- Provide you with pre-research orientation opportunities
- Provide you with other contacts that could result in job placement after graduation

These valuable people may be faculty or experienced doctorate candidates within your department; employees or experienced volunteers of local agencies; educators; or even small-business owners. Making an appointment to discuss their experiences can yield an amazing array of potential topics for your research. Scheduled at their convenience, these conversations will not be an imposition; people love talking about their passions.

Areas of specialty within your department

Most university websites not only list faculty and their research specialties but their recent publications as well. As you read through the titles of their recent research:

- Note any that grab your attention, including enough bibliographic information so you may locate the study at a later date.
- If the professor who wrote a noted study has tenure, place a star next to it because that professor's employment is likely to be stable.
- If you have enjoyed a course taught by the professor that wrote a noted study, place a star next to it.
- Record names of co-authors on the study, and find out if they are professors at another university or graduate students from yours.
- Take out your list from the previous section, and circle any topics that correspond to this recently published research.

The "Access to research" section of this chapter will discuss how you may access the studies you marked as most interesting.

Areas of interest from local agencies

Local agencies work tirelessly on a limited budget. They may have encountered problems or noticed trends they have neither the time nor the capacity to explore. You may already know nonprofits and government agencies that work in your field. Look them up in your telephone directory to see if they have local offices. If they do, make an appointment to:

- Introduce yourself as a graduate student interested in researching within their fields.
- Ask the simple question, "What would you like to know about _____ that you have not yet had time to pursue?"
- Ask additional questions to clarify, and probe the "why" of their curiosity.

If you do land such an appointment, make sure to dress appropriately, arrive on time, and take detailed notes. If you plan on using a voice recorder during the session, get permission ahead of time because voice recording carries an extra layer of liability for the person being interviewed. It also has the potential to limit the amount of useful information you might gather, so think hard about whether you want to use it. You may be best served with a simple notebook and pen.

Literature

Literature, in this context, is the entire body of knowledge within your discipline. It includes academic articles, theses and dissertations, books, interviews, conference proceedings, and archived audio-visual materials. Although you may be fascinated by everything in this knowledge storehouse, learn to limit your focus to the section that pertains to your topic.

Throughout your coursework, you doubtless had to read numerous research studies in preparation for exams and papers. So, by this time, you know where the library is and which section of the stacks your discipline resides. You have also most likely accessed articles electronically through your library's subscription account. Knowing where to find information is a valuable first step in the research process. But the next step in preparation for your thesis/dissertation is figuring out which information to look for.

Leading academic journals

Academic journals are peer-reviewed publications that serve as the core means of disseminating the latest findings from research all over the world. The standards imposed on scholarly articles appearing in these journals are rigorous to ensure the information is objective and significant. There is no shortage of information available. J-Stor® (**www.jstor.org**), a premiere electronic archive of academic journals, currently lists 226 titles in language and literature alone. Add to that 234 titles in the biological sciences, 167 titles in business, and 102 titles in mathematics and statistics, and you begin to see how you could spend the next decade in the library and still not even consume 10 percent of the knowledge within your field.

Fortunately, you do not have to. What you do have to accomplish is to find one topic, then one question within that topic to research. Because you do not yet know what your question will be, you will need to determine which journals are the best sources of information for your topic and begin reading the abstracts of articles from those journals. The top five will do. Here's how to know which ones are the best:

- Ask fellow graduate students.
- Take a quick tally from articles you read during courses that covered your topic.
- Visit the stacks at the library, and see which ones have the largest section.
- Enter your topic as a search term in your library's database, and see which journals come up most frequently.

There is no right or wrong in determining the leaders. They will entirely depend on your specific research focus. But, preparing yourself in this way for the review of literature will help you narrow down your search and maximize your reading time.

Other respected sources

A valuable source for topics is the library's store of theses and dissertations that have been completed through your department. In the last chapter of every thesis/dissertation is an "implications for future research" section. This section will discuss questions that came up during the research but were beyond the scope of the current study, as well as facets the researcher wished to look into but could not because of logistics. Request these rarely read sources, and mine the gold. The best part about finding topics from past student research is the likelihood of finding an adviser is high and the methodology is likely to be accessible to you.

Another source for topics is the monograph. *Merriam-Webster Online Dictionary* defines monographs as "a learned detailed treatise covering a small area of a field of learning." But, do not let the definition scare you away from reading them. Monographs are a terrific source of potential topics because their length and methodical nature allow them to describe interesting details that can be the starting points for your own brainstorming. Like theses and dissertations, they suggest new avenues for research toward the end. Monographs are sometimes bound separately like books or bundled in specialized monograph journals. If your library carries monographs, they will come up in a computerized search of the catalog. Some catalogs may even allow advanced searches in which you could specify publication type.

If you are fairly new to your discipline — for instance, seeking a graduate degree in a different field than your bachelor's degree — then reading an annual review is a must. Annual reviews are book-length surveys of the latest research topics for 40 disciplines, published by the nonprofit scientific publisher *Annual Reviews*. These reviews introduce research topics and cite leading pertinent studies. If your discipline is not covered by an annual review, search your library's catalog using the terms "literature review" and "[your topic]." The three most recent reviews should serve you well.

Access to research

Thanks to computers and the Internet, graduate students have easier access to research now than at any previous time in history. It is a rare day when a modern student arrives at the library with a zipper bag full of dimes to photocopy entire articles in microscopic two-pages-per-sheet settings to make the dimes last longer. Most universities pay for online subscriptions to journal archives, magazines, and newspapers, and they allow their students to access these documents via PDF files that may be downloaded onto zip drives or a laptop computer's hard drive.

As your topic turns into a specific research problem, however, you may find that a vital source is published in a journal your library does not carry. In that case, it is possible to order articles for a fee from a librarian or electronic archive. Spend your money wisely, though. Read through the abstracts before you buy, and only purchase the articles that truly pertain to your specific research problem.

Sometimes a key source is written in a language other than English. If you do not read that language, contact a professor from your university's foreign language department to arrange translation services from an experienced graduate student. If the language is not one taught by your university, contact the international student services on your campus; there may be students from appropriate countries who would translate your article for a fee. Make sure to arrange translation services before purchasing the article in question. You do not want to have the information in your hands and be unable to reach it.

ASSISTANCE: NETWORKING

Feelings of isolation are not uncommon in graduate school, especially during the writing stage of a thesis or dissertation. Some students work full time and squeeze in one or two classes per semester, racing on and off campus without stopping to network. With the proliferation of online classes, other students may not make it to campus at all for a semester. Still other students spend all their spare on-campus time in the library. Whether you fall into any of these categories, it is important to remember to connect with the people in your network. Your degree is preparing you for a career that will involve interaction with others. Partnership and collaboration are two important skills to learn during your program. Not only will these skills serve you well in your career, but they will also facilitate your journey through your thesis/dissertation and defense.

Graduate student groups

Scan the bulletin boards in your department for discipline-specific graduate student groups. Events such as writing workshops, journal discussion groups, or small-group seminars are great places to connect with fellow students. These groups are often organized by experienced, full-time graduate students who work on campus as research assistants or teaching assistants. They will have insight into your research topic, and they can advise you on politics within the department and faculty member quirks.

Other students' research

One of the best ways to prepare yourself for your own research is to assist others with theirs. Graduate students will rarely turn away free labor. If you have found a graduate student group, ask around to see if anyone needs help with data collection. Not only will you get a feel for various data-collection instruments and procedures, but you will also have prolonged interaction with a peer farther along in the process. This time will give you the chance to ask things you might have been too shy to ask before. If you work well together, you may even get a mentor out of the deal.

Potential advisers

Some programs assign advisers. If yours does not, you have an important decision to make. Do not make it lightly. A thesis/dissertation adviser can either facilitate or hamper progress toward graduation. An adviser's helpfulness is affected by numerous factors, including (but not limited to):

- **Familiarity with the chosen topic**. This will influence how much help your adviser can give you with content issues and sources.

- **Methodological skills**. This will affect how much help you can get from your adviser with research design, implementation, and analysis. If your adviser is not strong in this area, consultants are available.

- **Other on-campus responsibilities**. The number of teaching hours and administrative duties your adviser is assigned will impact how many hours he or she has to advise you and the ease/difficulty of scheduling meetings. The adviser's rate of publishing research will also impact his or her physical and mental availability.

- **Political savvy**. Advisers who know how to navigate their peer and administrative systems can insulate you from conflicts among faculty and can prevent you from blunders that could delay the approval of your research.

- **Stability in position**. If a professor is tenured, he or she has job security and can act on your behalf with more confidence. If a professor is tenure-track, he or she may hold back during committee meetings in fear of alienating tenured faculty.

- **Organizational habits**. If a professor has papers strewn across the desk, frequently rushes to the next appointment, and struggles to work on the most important things first, he or she is unlikely to hold you accountable for your requirements. He or she might even lose work you turn in for approval. If the professor at least uses an inbox and gets things done on time and in the right order, he or she can track your progress and help you meet your goals.

- **Personality conflicts with students and/or staff.** If a professor has a reputation for frequent arguments or grudges, you will find it difficult to operate under his or her supervision. Even if you get along with him or her, you may find that committee meetings become tense.

It is important to remember that time spent in graduate school is meant to prepare students for functioning as peers within the discipline. Part of that functioning will be the ability to survey a given situation and find ways to accomplish tasks within it. Although your journey through the graduate process will be more fun if you choose an adviser based on affability, you will not be able to choose your co-workers after graduation. Choosing an adviser based on familiarity with topic and research skills, even if said adviser is a little difficult, is a far better plan. In learning to navigate the needs and expectations of a quality researcher, despite any personality quirks, you will be prepared to work collaboratively and productively with your future colleagues.

If you surveyed the areas of specialty within your department described in the "Topic" section of this chapter, you already have a short list of potential advisers. Read through each candidate's latest article on the topic that interests you, and make an appointment to discuss his or her research and explore the possibility of working with him or her. *The "Written Work" section of this chapter lists elements to include in this appointment request.* Remember that you will be asking someone to be your adviser, but the professor you ask is not obligated to say yes. Be professional and courteous at all times during these interviews to make the best impression.

Support services

Universities vary, but yours should have some version of the following types of on-campus assistance. Use your university's website and on-campus directory to make a contact list for yourself. Record the name, location, and phone number of the following services that apply to your situation:

- Tutoring and study skills assistance
- Writing center
- Off-campus and nontraditional student services
- Applicable student organizations
- Accessibility services
- Veterans assistance
- Diversity affairs
- International student services
- Advocacy services
- On-campus child care
- Health services

Even if you never use these services, knowing they exist will ease anxiety. Plus, if you are pursuing your graduate degree on a part-time basis, your needs and life situation may alter significantly over the five or more years your degree takes. Keep this list in a safe place to save yourself time later on.

DATA: LEARNING TO USE IT

For the purposes of this book, the term data include all information collected and analyzed in exploration of your research problem. Depending on your research design, your data may include numerical measurements or written information. Both are valid forms of data overall, but you will eventually work with your adviser to determine which type is most appropriate for your research problem.

Your department's statistics course

If your department requires all graduate students to take a statistics course and you have not already taken it, do it now — even if you plan to avoid number crunching in your thesis/dissertation. The introduction to statistical concepts will be integral to understanding the vast number of research studies you are about to read. It will also dispel some of the mystery of statistics within your discipline so you remain open to numerical approaches. Having an open mind will make your research more robust and will make discussions with your adviser more pleasant during the design phase.

Here is more food for thought. Charles Coleman and Cynthia Conrad published a study in 2007 on math anxiety in graduate students. Through a combination of literature review and data collection, they found that statistics avoidance resulted in:

- Missed class hours
- Impaired ability to finish programs
- Impaired engagement in academic careers and research

You have already invested an immense amount of time and effort to get this far. It would be a shame to let math anxiety, or even just math dislike, derail your plans. Sign up for statistics. Go to class. Find a tutor if you have to — just complete the course.

Realistic expectations of your role in data analysis

Unless you are pursuing your degree in statistics, you are not expected to become an expert statistician while writing your thesis/dissertation. What you are expected to do is learn how to design, execute, and analyze research. Your adviser and committee will be there to help you along the way. The type of analysis chosen for your thesis/dissertation will be affected by your:

- Research focus — appropriate to your research problem
- Aptitude — comprehension is vital to interpreting the results
- Personality — appropriate to your predilection for detail
- Experience — with statistics previously

Research perspectives

There are two basic types of research perspectives — qualitative and quantitative — divided by underlying philosophies about reality. Understanding the difference between the two will help you during discussions with your adviser while you develop your research problem. To aid in that understanding, the two approaches will be defined below. Then, when you read journal articles, you will be encouraged to identify which approach each study takes. *See Chapter 2 for more information about using these research methods.* Be aware that there are studies that incorporate a blend of the two perspectives.

A qualitative approach to research involves the gathering of data in the form of observations and other written information because reality is relative and influenced by perception. Qualitative approaches are frequently used to research the history of, trends in, and theories about a topic. Case studies are qualitative research focused on a narrow subject. Interviews, focus groups, and direct observations also can employ a qualitative approach to research. Although many qualitative approaches may not involve complex statistical analyses, there are qualitative studies that assign codes to the information collected in order to look for patterns.

For example, a researcher might follow the lives of three drug-addicted teens, following their rehabilitation over the course of two years and interviewing them about school, home, and future goals on a quarterly basis. Teen 1 stayed clean, graduated from high school, and enrolled in a local college. Teen 2 stayed clean but dropped out of school and now works full time at a restaurant. Teen 3 relapsed, returned to rehabilitation, and now attends an alternative education center. The researcher might analyze the notes to look for any similarities between Teen 1 and 2 that differ from Teen 3 in order to find a possible predictor of rehabilitation success then suggest in the discussion section that another researcher test this predictor using quantitative methods.

A quantitative approach to research involves the gathering of data in the form of numerical values because reality is objective and measurable. Quantitative approaches are frequently used in studies involving experiments, the correlation/difference between two or more factors, and the search for causal factors to various phenomena. Although quantitative approaches record fine-grained detail about the specific items measured, they are limited in their ability to take other observations into the analysis.

For instance, in a study of the difference that water level makes in the growth of a plant, a researcher may choose to measure plants' height and width. But, over the course of the study, the researcher may notice that some plants are darker green than others. Because measurement of color was not included in the methodology, the only thing the researcher can do is mention the difference during the conclusion section as a possible avenue to pursue in future research.

TYPES OF RESEARCH

As with research perspectives, understanding the differences between research types and knowing which types work best within your topic will help you as you plan your own project. Pull out the recent articles written by professors in your department before you read through the following descriptions, and try to identify which research type those studies used. As you will see, the choice of research type depends on the research problem in question.

Descriptive

Descriptive studies work best when researching a problem for which little is known. The goal of descriptive studies is to gain enough familiarity with the topic to learn where and how to focus more detailed research in the future. Descriptive research uses a quantitative approach to gather data in order to calculate averages, percentages, and frequencies. No causal factors or relationships may be ascertained but merely a description of traits and trends. Common examples of studies using descriptive designs are:

- Natural histories
- Classifications or re-classifications of phenomena
- Identification of social trends

Correlational

Correlational studies search for relationships between factors. They make and test predictions of one variable's performance based on the performance of another variable. This correlation does not equal causation. Variables found to be significantly correlated would need to be studied further with a causal-comparative approach before such a conclusion could be drawn. A positive correlation means the factors being compared change in the same direction — for example, as one rises so does the other. A negative correlation means these factors change in opposite directions — for example, as one increases the other decreases. If the correlation coefficient is zero, then researchers conclude no correlation between the factors exists.

Causal-comparative

Causal-comparative research is an after-the-fact search for causation of phenomena. It focuses on the state of variables as they occur naturally as opposed to being manipulated through experimentation. Because the study subjects must be found after the phenomena have occurred, random assignment of subjects to groups is not possible. This places a strong burden on the researcher to carefully plan the makeup of each study group and thoroughly describe the study subjects, especially if there is hope of generalizing findings to other groups.

Experimental

Experimental designs work best when researching problems involving cause and effect. Use of control groups, well-defined manipulation of experimental groups, and random assignment of subjects into groups are characteristics of this research type. Experimental research uses a quantitative approach to gather data via measurements of pre-defined variables, looking for statistically significant differences between the experimental and control groups. Common examples of studies using experimental designs are:

- Double-blind (meaning the researcher and the group being studied do not know the conditions of the experiment), placebo-controlled pharmaceutical studies
- Animal behavior experiments
- Stress tolerance of construction materials

Quasi-experimental

Quasi-experimental designs are similar to experimental designs, except they do not use random assignment of subjects into groups. These studies are common in educational research, in which student safety and teacher cooperation make true random assignment and double-blind designs difficult to implement. Instructional hours are jealously guarded so nondistrict educational researchers look for classes that already fit the criteria for their different study groups so data may be collected with little to no impact on the children's typical schedule.

WRITTEN WORK: INTRODUCTION

Because this chapter is about preparation rather than accomplishment, there will be few tasks from this section. But, it is important to orient yourself now to the purpose of the vast written task you are about to undertake. As noted in previous sections, you will find sample wordings for letters of introduction to potential advisers and employees of local agencies. These letters should be a top priority to move on to the next phase of your paper as soon as possible.

Function and scope

The function of the thesis and dissertation is to prepare students to enter into meaningful dialogue with members of their planned profession and contribute new ideas. Both projects teach students how to access the literature of their disciplines and absorb and evaluate the contents. However, the thesis serves as an introduction to the discipline and is conducted at an apprentice level. Students completing a thesis are expected to know the elements of quality research and how to access assistance in research design. In contrast, the dissertation is intended to turn the writer into an academic peer. Students completing a dissertation are expected to know how to design research and analyze the quality of others' research. Dissertation research is conducted at a level that demonstrates mastery of topic and methodology and proves the doctoral candidate is worthy of the title, its responsibilities, and its benefits.

Letters of introduction to potential advisers

Whether you have taken classes from the possible professorial candidates for the privilege of being your adviser (for example, the professors who wrote the three studies you selected in the "Assistance" section), take the time to introduce yourself properly and in writing before meeting with them to drop the big question. Real letters are a rarity in this electronic world, so make a nice impression and print this letter on quality paper with proper correspondence formatting. This sends a message that you understand and value the importance of the adviser/advisee relationship. A quick follow-up on the letter with a phone call or e-mail is encouraged to make sure they received and/or read the letter because professors tackle stacks of paper every day.

This letter should include:

1. A salutation. "Dear [Professor/Dr.] _____,". If you are already on a first-name basis with these professors, then use first names in the letters.

2. A compliment referring to a facet of his or her research that relates to the topics you are considering. "I enjoyed reading your article in [name of journal] that reported [significant finding]."

3. A statement of your response to the article. "After reading it, I began to wonder if [altered variable, subject, or procedure] would significantly change the outcome."

4.   A statement of your desire to discuss the article. "If you have the time in the next two weeks, I would really like to make an appointment with you to discuss your research further."

5.   Notification that you are in the process of seeking a topic. "Because I am nearly finished with my coursework, I am exploring various research options for my [thesis/dissertation]."

6.   A statement of gratitude for the sacrifice of time this meeting will mean. "I realize you are very busy with teaching and research already. But, if you could spare the time, I would really appreciate it."

7.   A signature. "Sincerely, [the name the professor knows you by]" followed by a statement of where he or she met you if needed.

Approaching these professors in writing makes a good impression, and it gives you an insurance policy against any potential slips of the tongue because of nerves. Everything you truly need them to know is in the letter. So, if you run into them in the hall, you do not have to worry about forgetting something or jumping straight to the end and scaring them off. You have more time to organize your thoughts in a letter than in any verbal scenario. Even if you talk to these professors all the time, the formality of your intention is bound to throw a little stammer or tremor into a verbal pitch.

Requests for interviews with local agencies

The same benefits of facilitating a good first impression apply to your interview requests with the local agencies you identified in the "Topic" section of this chapter. But, here the importance of first impression is even greater. Professors at your university must at least consider giving you their time, as it is part of their job. Professionals and volunteers of local agencies do not have that same obligation. Your letter of introduction must also convince them that spending time on you will benefit them more than spending that time on their usual tasks.

This letter should include:

1. A salutation. "Dear [Mr./Ms./Dr.] _____," unless you are already on a first-name basis.

2. Notification that you are a graduate student exploring various research options. "My name is _____, and I am a graduate student at [name of university]. I am currently exploring various research options for my [thesis/dissertation]."

3. A compliment regarding the work of the agency that pertains to a research topic you are exploring, along with how you found out about it. "I recently read in [name of paper, blog, pamphlet, website] that [name of agency] succeeded in _____."

4. A statement of your response to that work. "I applaud that because _____."

5. A statement of your desire to discuss that work. "If you have the time in the next two weeks, I would really like to make an appointment with you to discuss [agency's current work], including any facets you think could use further study."

6. A statement of gratitude for the sacrifice of time this meeting will mean. "I realize you are very busy with your current responsibilities, but if you could spare the time, I would be most grateful."

7. A signature. "Sincerely, [your legal name]" followed by your contact information, including mobile phone if applicable.

Following up with a phone call to the office within a week after you think the letter arrived is advised. If your letter went straight into the circular file, the office staff will likely give you a polite brush off, and you will know to go elsewhere. But, if your letter went into a stack of interesting-yet-not-urgent correspondence, your phone call will be seen as a welcome display of professional drive and courtesy.

STAYING ORGANIZED

If you have been doing the tasks in this chapter as you go, then you have already made a list of topics, collected research articles, made notes regarding research perspectives and types, and written letters of introduction. Where did you store these items? How long would it take you to find them and look at them? Write down your estimate, and time yourself while you actually pull them out. Do not read further until you have done this.

How long did it actually take you? If it took you longer than five minutes, then your current organizational system needs some tweaking before you go any further in your thesis/dissertation process. The following section will help you design an organizational system and disaster recovery plan that will keep you productive and on track from design through defense.

Organizational media

Whether you are a traditional paper person or an electronic gadget junkie, your system will most likely involve some type of media you prefer not to deal with. But, taking the time and leaving your comfort zone now will prepare you for dealing with the materials you will have to track in your new career. Remember that your thesis/dissertation is not an end unto itself. It is a beginning. Take the time to develop a system that works for you, and solidify the habit of using it.

Paper documentation

Even if you prefer an all-electronic work flow, there will be administrative forms and correspondence you will have to track and file along the way. You may even prefer taking notes in a bona fide notebook with a real pencil or pen in your hand. Whatever your style, be sure your plan implements some form of the following:

- **Notebook or paper pad**. For most research, keeping a pad of paper handy is a good idea for jotting down notes, diagramming thoughts, and making to-do lists. This pad can be whatever style and size you prefer; if you like seeing and touching it, you will be more likely to use it. If your research takes you to field sites, you might want to use a tape-bound notebook instead and journal your trips. This ensures your chronology of observations stays intact.

- **File folders**, preferably with tabs for easy reference. Be sure to label them in specific terms so one folder does not contain too many documents. File folders are best for items that need to be kept in pristine condition, such as forms, contracts, and important correspondence. Store these file folders in a system that works for you: file cabinet, portable file box, binders, or rolling briefcase.

- **4-inch binder**. This will be the home of all your paper research materials, including photocopied literature sources, hand-written notes, sketches, data instruments and records, analysis output, drafts of tables and graphs, and hard copies of visual media. Insert tabbed dividers so all materials for each key concept are grouped together. Decide whether you will organize the materials within each tab alphabetically or chronologically, then three-hole punch the materials and insert. During the writing phase, you will be glad you are flipping through a binder instead of juggling loose papers. Depending on your budget and comfort level with electronic media, you may substitute this with a portable scanner and laptop. *See the "Electronic" section in this chapter for more electronic resource ideas.*

- **2-inch binder**. This will be the home of your current proposal and thesis/dissertation draft. Insert tabbed dividers for each chapter of the written work. Carry this binder with you whenever you are on campus in case your adviser or committee member flags you down for an impromptu discussion.

Electronic documentation

Even if you prefer an all-paper workflow, there will be elements of your thesis/dissertation you will have to do electronically. Word processing is a must now, not to mention the crisp results that software gives to graphs and tables. Statistical analysis is rarely computed by hand; some data are even collected electronically, with probes and push buttons sending information to computers. The best thing about electronic organizational systems is the amount of information they can store in a small space. In addition to the paper organization you developed above, organize your electronic information using some version of the following:

- **Folders**. On your computer, make sure to set up a separate thesis/dissertation folder within your Documents folder. For now, make separate folders within the thesis/dissertation folder for each topic you explore, and move any files pertaining to those topics into those folders. As you make your topic choice and develop your research problem, set up a folder for each chapter of your thesis/dissertation, as well as a folder for each pertinent keyword. This way, PDF copies of journal articles, data files, word processing drafts, and many other electronic materials will be a quick click away at all times.

- **Laptop computer and portable scanner**. If you prefer a mostly electronic workflow, this may be the best way to store and track the bulk of your research materials. Notes, photocopied sources, and anything else on sheets of paper can be scanned and stored in the file system described above, which ensures you always have the information you need in a predictable location. This may be substituted with a 4-inch binder; see the previous "Paper" section.

- **Bibliographic file**. Storing your bibliographic data electronically from the start will save you time and frustration during the writing stage. Using a spreadsheet or database to populate a bibliography template within your manuscript will allow you to rearrange your sources at every stage of the drafting process and update formatting if style changes are requested by your committee. *See the "Software" section that follows for instructions on how to do this with Microsoft® Office and OpenOffice™ software.*

- **Flash drive or portable external hard drive.** These are pocket-sized devices that connect to computers via the USB port. They contain anywhere from 1 to 500 gigabytes of memory and cost less than $100. Flash drives are handy for storing a limited number of files until you can transfer them to your home computer, for instance, when downloading articles using the library's computer or running a statistical analysis in the university's computer lab. External hard drives, on the other hand, can often store every file you need for the entirety of your project, thus making your files available from any computer you have access to.

Physical samples

Depending on your research problem, you may have specimens or data-collection instruments that need to be stored and produced during presentations of your work. Make sure to find a safe, moisture-controlled, temperature-controlled location to store these items. Obtain containers that will protect them from damage and make them easily transportable. Label the containers with the collection date(s), collection location(s), and any other necessary identifiers. Before placing samples in long-term storage, make sure to photograph them with a digital camera. Things happen — it is better to have a backup image than nothing at all during your defense.

Common organizational software

Using office software to compose and edit your notes and documents will save you time and effort. Information will only have to be entered once and will allow you to copy, paste, or import that information into other locations in different formats. If you do not have access to the Microsoft Office suite, you can download a free OpenOffice suite from **www.openoffice.org** for

Windows, Mac, and Linux operating systems. The most common types of software you will use during the writing and defending of your thesis/dissertation are:

- Word processor, such as Microsoft Word or OpenOffice Writer. Use word-processing software to compose and edit text, tables, bibliographies, and correspondence.

- Spreadsheet, such as Microsoft Excel or OpenOffice Calc. Use spreadsheet software to store research results and bibliographic information, run simple calculations, and populate tables and templates.

- Presentation, such as Microsoft PowerPoint or OpenOffice Impress. Use presentation software to prepare and present multimedia slide shows for your proposal and defense.

- Database, such as Microsoft Access or OpenOffice Base. Use a database only if you have to, as the setup is complex. If you have large quantities of multivariate data, a database may be a possibility for you, but find someone with experience in setting up queries to help you.

Depending on the statistical analysis your research problem requires, you may also need to learn how to use statistical software. Access to and use of this software should be explained during your department's statistics course. Your adviser may have preferred software as well.

Digital audio/visual devices

Digital audio/visual devices allow quick capture of information in an ultra-portable package.

If you are working in the life sciences, you may need to record images and/or audio of your study organisms for recall during the writing phase and for impact during your defense. If you are in a meeting with your adviser, and you worked out an elegant flow chart on the white board, you can capture it before it gets erased for the next brainstorm. If you have been reading for hours and then think of something brilliant during the ten minutes you had planned to rest, you can record a voice memo with your eyes closed. The list goes on.

Nearly all mobile phones now come with a built-in voice recorder and camera, and some even have video capability. Even if you need better quality or larger storage capacity, single-purpose devices such as digital cameras and voice recorders can still slip in a pocket or handbag. If you are going to purchase one of these devices, look for models that use SD (secure digital) cards or mini-SD cards. SD cards are the small, square-shaped removable memory cards that allow users to access digital files without having to plug the actual recording device into the computer. Many computers now come with SD card slots, which makes it simple and convenient to transfer your media files into your organizational system, thus preventing cameras and voice recorders from getting fried in power surges.

The trick is organizing the output from digital devices to avoid loss from misfiling or forgetfulness. Using one of the cloud-computing options listed above will ensure you can take full advantage of your media files as long as you remain disciplined about entering the files into your organizational system.

New ways of staying organized

The goal of technology, in regard to research, is to enter a given piece of information once in such a way as to make it accessible in numerous forms. For instance, in the days of typewriters, graduate students were forced to retype every draft from scratch. Many unaltered sentences were retyped five or more times before the defense because other portions of that page changed. Now that word processing software is common, you only need to retype the revised portions. This same concept applies to files, search engine queries, and audio-visual materials.

Cloud computing

Cloud computing is a relatively new concept; the term itself was launched in 2007 in preparation for an information-technology (IT) conference called Cloud Expo. What it means for small business is outsourcing IT needs without having to worry about scalability, reliability, and recovery. What it means for you is a new range of Web applications to manipulate and store information you gather that is more resistant to loss by human error, virus attack, and natural disaster than in-home options. Some cloud computing options you have access to are:

- Google™ docs, a free Web application that allows you to create, store, search, and share word-processing documents, spreadsheet documents, and online forms. To use this service, visit **http:// docs.google.com** from any Web browser on any operating system. Sign in with your Google account. Click the "get started" button if you do not have one. If you have a Gmail™, Blogger, or YouTube account, you may already have a Google account without realizing it. Once you accept the terms of service, you will have your own little patch of cloud. Although you are now able to upload any file type to store and share in Google docs, you are still limited in your ability to edit. Word-processing documents and spreadsheets are converted to the Google docs format prior to editing online. If your document contains large amounts of special formatting, this may not be the editing solution you want to use.

- Dropbox, a variable-rate Web application that allows you to store, share, and synchronize any file type. Your first 2 gigabytes of storage are free, with bonus storage added when friends accept your invitation to join. To use this service, visit **www.dropbox.com** from your Windows, Mac, or Linux home computer, and click on the "get Dropbox" button. Installation instructions vary depending on your operating system, but Dropbox walks you through them with adequate directions. If you have an iPhone or iPod Touch, you may want to install the Dropbox app as well. When you install Dropbox on a computer, it creates a Dropbox folder. Any file you save to that folder will automatically synchronize with your Dropbox folder in the "cloud." Any time that file is edited, the cloud version will be updated automatically. It is like having a continuous backup running. Files can be accessed and manually updated from any Internet-connected computer by logging in to your account on the Dropbox website.

• Evernote®, a variable-rate Web application that allows you to capture, store, tag, and search a variety of media. The free account allows you to upload 500 megabytes of notes, .pdf and .txt files, pictures, voice memos, and Web-based content. For $5 per month (less if you pay a year in advance), you can upload any file type and increase your storage capacity. To use this service, visit **www. evernote.com** from your Windows or Mac computer. Evernote also has utilities for various mobile devices. Installation instructions vary by device, but they are not complicated. When you install Evernote on your computer, it will allow you to capture information with a simple right-click and selection of "add to Evernote." Evernote on your mobile device will allow you to capture information with the device's camera or microphone or simply type a text-based note. You can even e-mail information to your Evernote system. Synchronization is manual.

Social media to create discussion

Speaking of discipline, social media can be an excellent way to record and discuss quick thoughts about your research — *if* you can stay on task and not get lost in a sea of celebrity gossip. None of the following suggestions are meant to convince you to start regularly using social media; they are merely ideas in case you already enjoy blogging, tweeting on Twitter™, or conversing on Facebook®.

- Post a short (50- to 150-word) "find of the week" on your blog that describes an interesting fact or surprising discovery, including appropriate links and pictures. These should not be major results but quirky or fun bits that will add texture and depth to your thesis/dissertation's final chapter. End each post with a question if you would like to get feedback from others interested in your topic.

- Post "find of the week" notes on your Facebook wall, similar to the blog posts suggested above. You might also start an album in which you upload pictures of yourself preparing for or conducting your research; be sure these pictures will not violate another person's privacy. This is a great way to seek encouragement and moral support. Plus, writing short captions in everyday language will help you develop ways of making your research relevant to the public. If you choose to make these Facebook albums public (viewable by everyone, not just friends), they could make a great impression with potential employers or other researchers in your topic — just make sure you adjust the privacy settings of any potentially embarrassing photos to be "friends only."

- If you are using Evernote to track your files (as mentioned in the previous "Cloud computing" section) and you have a Twitter account, consider linking the two accounts. This will allow you to use a mobile phone to text short thoughts and memos into Evernote for processing later. To do this, follow "myEN" from your Twitter account. Evernote will send you a direct message (DM). Click on the link in that direct message, sign in to your Evernote account, then click to link the accounts. When you successfully complete these steps, you may either DM private notes to myEN or add @myEN to public notes. These tweets will automatically route to your Evernote account, where you may tag and edit them.

Saved searches and e-mail alerts

Search engines, such as Google and Yahoo!®, have made the task of finding current information easier than any other time in history. Although not all the information these search engines call up is accurate, the list of links they generate can alert you to trends and news items related to your topic. Quickly scan the results and look for relevance in the title and the page summaries before clicking through. Only spend your time on high quality links that have major relevance. If you would like recurring e-mail notifications about new Web-based content related to your topic, you may save your search through the following services:

- **Google Alerts**. Visit **www.google.com/alerts**, and type your topic in the "search term" box. Use whichever combination of words gave you the highest-quality results in previous searches. Customize your alert by using the dropdown boxes below the search box. Choose the type of Web content you want included (such as blogs, news, and video), how often you want to be notified, how long the list of results should be, and the e-mail address you would like the results delivered to. Make sure to click on the "create alert" button when you are through.

- **Yahoo**! **Alerts**. Visit **http://alerts.yahoo.com**, and click on "keyword news." Type your topic in the "include" box, using the most successful combination of words from previous searches. Specify how often you want to be notified and the e-mail address you would like the results delivered to. Make sure to click on the "save alert" button when you finish.

If you use Twitter, you can save a search through the user interface as well. However, using this feature for thesis/dissertation research is not recommended, as you will most likely not be able to keep up with the volume and pace of information pouring in, not to mention the difficulty in determining which leads are quality leads.

ORGANIZATION: ESTABLISHING YOUR SYSTEM

Now that you have reviewed the various media and devices at your disposal, it is time to develop your personal system. By this point, you have probably identified which of the above items work best for you, so it is just a matter of planning where and how you will store information from all the different contexts you will encounter. Answering the questions within the following overview of contexts will help you set up an organizational cheat sheet so you never have to wonder where to store something, thus maximizing access to and preventing loss of vital information.

Deadlines

Some of the deadlines you encounter will be personal, some administrative. All your important dates — appointments and deadlines — should be stored in the same location to avoid conflicts. Before you have a load of deadlines to track, ask yourself the following questions:

- Where do I currently store my appointments and deadlines?
- How often do I check that place?
- Where would I be more likely to check for appointments and deadlines (if checking stated location less than once a day)?
- Do I frequently miss or nearly miss these deadlines?
- What kind of supports could I put into place to manage my time better (if missing deadlines)?

Contact information

Throughout the thesis/dissertation process, you will meet and interact with people. These people are necessary for completing your degree, and they are also necessary for building a professional network. Storing contact information in a functional location as you go, rather than scrambling for information during an emergency, will facilitate a smooth research process and your transition from student to colleague. Before you organize the contacts you already have and gather new ones, ask yourself the following questions:

- How do I gather contact information?
- Where do I currently store contact information?

- Am I storing addresses, phone numbers, e-mail addresses, and websites in the same place?
- What is a typical length of time that I search for a phone number? An e-mail address? A physical address?
- Where could I store this information so it takes me fewer than 45 seconds to access it?

Drafts

Between the time you type the first word of your proposal and the last word of your final thesis/dissertation version, you will have generated at least ten printed drafts distributed to your adviser and/or committee. The last thing you want during the precious discussion time you have with them is to be talking in circles because one of you is referencing an outdated draft. To prevent this confusion, ask yourself the following questions:

- Do I edit my own work better on paper or on the computer screen?
- How will I distinguish my own working drafts from a draft that will be distributed to my committee (if self-editing on paper)?
- How will I distinguish distributed draft versions so I can quickly tell if someone is looking at the wrong one?
- Where will I store the most current draft?
- Will I store previously distributed drafts? If so, where?

Meeting notes and methodology

Meetings with advisers, committee members, and local experts are valuable sources of information, not all of which can be absorbed at the time of the meeting. You will need a way to capture and store the information generated by these meetings in a format that is functional for you and comfortable for others, especially while designing your methodology with your adviser. Prior to each meeting, ask yourself the following questions:

- How will I capture visual information at this meeting? Where will I store it?

- How will I capture auditory information at this meeting? Where will I store it?

- How will I capture printed information at this meeting? Where will I store it?

- Do I have a valid reason for wanting to record audio or video at this meeting? Will any attendees object? If so, what are my alternatives?

- How will I make sure I can quickly access notes that pertain to a particular facet of my research?

Citing Sources

Misplacing sources is a massive threat to successfully defending a scholarly work. During the design phase, an adviser may pose a problem that triggers the vague notion of a solution-containing source, but after hours of digging, no source can be found, and the solution is delayed. During the writing phase, a remembered line from a source may fit perfectly, but then the exact wording cannot be found and the point must be left unsupported. During the preparation of the bibliography, a referenced source disappears so the citation cannot be made and the reference must be removed. These are all nightmares, yet they are all preventable nightmares.

The sources cited in your thesis/dissertation will be fluid during the research and writing process, so the best method for tracking and reporting them is with computer software. This will not only help you keep an ever-changing list of sources alphabetized, but it will also help you correct formatting errors without the need to retype the entire list. The two most accessible options for this are using the mail merge option in the Microsoft Office suite and the bibliography database option in the OpenOffice suite. Below are instructions for the entry of bibliographic data for both methods. *Instructions for populating your bibliography with that data will be covered in Chapter 5.*

Microsoft Office method:

1.   Open a new Excel spreadsheet.

2.   In line No. 1 column A, type "source #" and then tab to the next column.

3.   Enter the rest of your headers in successive columns. Headers should correspond to each element needed to properly reference your sources. A starting list of headers should include authors, year published, article/chapter title, journal/book title, pages, city, URL, and keywords.

4.   Choose File > Save As, navigate to the folder you want to save your file in, give your file a name, and click "save."

5.   To begin entering information for your first source, assign it a source number. You may choose your own numbering system: in the order you find them, coded with the date you found them, coded with the location you found them, or anything else that makes sense to you. Type the first source number in line 2 column A, then tab to the next column.

6.   Type the authors in line 2 column B. Format the authors' names the way they will need to appear in the bibliography — check your department's preferred style guide. A common format is: Author 1 [Last, First], Author 2 [First Last], and Author 3 [First Last].

7.   Continue entering the elements in the remainder of the columns. Hit the enter key to move to the next line for the next source.

8.   Make sure to save your file.

OpenOffice method:

1.   Read the "Bibliographies" article by Don Peterson on the Tutorials for OpenOffice website before you begin (**www.tutorialsforopenoffice.org/tutorial/Bibliographies.html**).

This overview of the process is a must for navigating this process right the first time so you will save time and effort when generating your bibliographies at the end.

2.   Open a new Writer document.

3.   Choose Tools > Bibliography Database. The database will open pre-filled with some sources as examples. You will not need to delete these.

4.   To begin entering information for your first source, assign it a source number (see "Microsoft Office method, step 5"). Notice the form in the bottom half of the screen. Type the first source number in the "short name" box.

5.   Fill in as much of the information in the rest of the form as your source has, using the tab key to move from box to box.

6.   Click the square button with a yellow sun in it to start entering a new source.

7.   There is no need to save; it is done automatically when you tab to the next box.

8.   Make sure to follow the tutorial instructions for tagging statements in your proposal and thesis/dissertation that need to be cited.

Data and analysis

Your analysis and conclusions will only be as good as your data. Taking careful notes about what data-collection methods and analyses are used in the literature will help you bring quality suggestions to design meetings. Recording and entering data on the same day will ensure accuracy. Keeping detailed notes about the circumstances surrounding data collection will give you insight when interpreting the results of your analysis, especially if things did not go exactly as planned. Data loss can potentially deal a fatal blow to degree completion so make sure the sun never sets without making a backup copy of your data and/or analysis output. Now ask yourself:

- How will I capture data? Where will I store it?
- How will I analyze the data (software versus hand calculation)? Where will I store the results?
- How will I create and store backups? *See the next section.*

YOUR RECOVERY PLAN

Disaster is inevitable. The size and impact of disasters vary, but all are frustrating and potentially degree threatening. The first type of disaster is research related; something may go wrong with the execution of your research. It will take a team effort between you and your committee to solve this type of disaster; know that loss of study population or negative experimental results are all workable with some creative thinking and an open mind.

The second type of disaster is data related — something may go wrong with the information you gathered from your research. Data in this case refer to every piece of information associated with the designing, writing, and defending of your thesis/dissertation. Developing a plan for data recovery now and routinely executing that plan as you go will prevent this type of disaster from threatening your degree. The concept behind this plan is simple: multiple copies in multiple places. Single copies are vulnerable to theft, loss, or destruction. But, making copies does not mean making exact replicas. A copy could be made via photographs, photocopies, scans, videos, or any other digital means. A great habit would be to make copies of each day's research by the end of the day. A good habit would be to make copies of the week's research at the end of each week. Remember that no plan works unless it is carried out routinely. To develop your disaster-recovery plan, ask yourself the following questions:

- Where will I store my paper data originals?
- Will I scan, photocopy, or photograph that data for copies?

- In case of natural disaster, is there some place I can store these copies that is at least 100 miles away?

- If so, how would I get the copies there? How often could I do this?

- Where will I store my electronic data files?

- Will I use a CD/DVD or external hard drive to make a local copy? How often?

- Which cloud-based service will I use to make a remote copy? How often?

- How will I retrieve my data in the event of catastrophic loss?

CASE STUDY: STARTING OFF RIGHT – CHOOSING YOUR ADVISER AND CREATING A SUPPORT SYSTEM

Corey Muench
Instructor, Capilano University

BIOGRAPHY:

Corey Muench completed a dual M.A. in French linguistics and applied linguistics at Indiana University in Bloomington. He currently teaches in the ESL Department at Capilano University in Vancouver, British Columbia, Canada.

THESIS TITLE AND SYNOPSIS:

Attention, Strategies, and the Role of Instruction in Second Language Phonological Acquisition

The study included 15 adult, non-native speakers of English who were enrolled in an English pronunciation course. Through a questionnaire, personal interviews, and recorded dialogue journals, the researcher examined the amount of attention learners paid to their pronunciation improvement, the types of strategies used, and the effect of instruction on their attention and strategies.

Results showed that instruction had the effect of sorting out confusing or inaccurate information, revealing key information not previously taught (even to learners at an advanced level), fostering the noticing of newly learned pronunciation features in everyday ambient language, and encouraging self-analysis of pronunciation output. The course also gave learners a realistic idea of their own pronunciation limitations.

FIRST-PERSON ACCOUNT:

In my M.A. program, there was a choice of a thesis or an exam. I chose the thesis option because I felt that doing a research study would give me a head start for my Ph.D. dissertation. This was actually a smart plan because once I did begin the dissertation, I was able to build on my M.A. thesis and planned to use some of the data collected there.

However, after I did some work on my dissertation, I did not finish the Ph.D. The major reason I didn't finish was because when I began the Ph.D., I had a much too idealistic view of what I could and should accomplish in life. I did not fully realize that my first love is teaching and developing teaching materials, *not* doing research. Had I followed those true desires, I never would have started a Ph.D.

I do believe, though, that writing a thesis [for my M.A.] instead of doing a comprehensive exam was a good choice. In addition to preparing me for later research, it gave me the option of actually publishing something, it taught me how to conduct a real study, and it taught me the pitfalls of research involving human subjects. I feel that cramming for comprehensive exams would have just given me factual knowledge I would have later forgotten.

I have two tips for graduate students on how to write a successful thesis/dissertation. First, make sure your thesis/dissertation topic is one your adviser is interested in and knows something about. If your adviser does not have much experience with your topic, you will not be able to get as much involvement and advice, no matter how hard you try. Instead, you will be following a lonely path and receive little input on key decisions. Even if your adviser is enthusiastic about helping out, she or he may simply not have enough knowledge of the topic. University professors have very little time to help out, but if they are interested in your topic, they will be more likely to pay attention to you because your findings could have a positive impact on their own work.

Second, support groups are invaluable. While I was working on my dissertation, I joined a dissertation support group organized by the campus counseling office. This group brought together graduate students from a wide range of departments. I learned I was not the only one going through similar problems, and we used each other as motivators to complete weekly tasks. At each meeting, we would update the group on our progress. This may seem stressful, but support groups are there for just that — support. If I had not completed a planned task, the group just asked me to explore why it did not get done. In general, the group was great for offering motivation, setting goals, identifying strategies to overcome problems, and providing camaraderie. Every time I left the meeting, I felt that a load had been lifted from my shoulders.

SUMMARY OF TASKS

Phase 1

- Make a list of potential topics.
- Survey local research problems.
- Familiarize yourself with leading sources in your discipline.
- Network.
- Take statistics.

Phase 2

- Write letters of introduction to potential advisers and local experts.
- Design your organizational system.
- Design your disaster-recovery system.

Chapter 2: Explore

With an orientation to topics of interest in your field and a functional organization system in place, it is now time to choose one topic and explore it. A vast array of research problems already wait for you within your chosen topic; the trick is choosing one and sticking with it — a task made simpler by obtaining an adviser. This chapter will equip you with the tools you need to ask the most appropriate person to be your adviser and develop a positive working relationship with him or her. Because of the nonlinear nature of the tasks in this chapter, you may want to read it completely through once before you begin the exploration phase.

TOPIC: CHOOSING A SPECIFIC PROBLEM

In the previous chapter, you made a list of three potential topics. Take that list out now, and, if you have not already, choose which topic you will research. Remember that this is not your specific research problem but merely the more focused area within your discipline. Use whichever criteria meet your needs best: comprehension, feasibility, accessibility of assistance, and/or preference. Discussing your options with someone over a meal might help you if you are struggling to decide. A good friend or close family member might be able to spot your subconscious preferences from body language or word choice as you talk, and clue you in. Do not move on in this chapter until you have chosen a topic.

Now that you have chosen your topic, it is time to work toward your specific research problem. This process can take days to weeks, depending on the speed with which you find an adviser and your background knowledge in the topic. All new research flows from previous research, so do not be overly concerned with finding something completely original. You can conduct solid research that adds a piece of information to the global body of knowledge about your topic if you:

- **Replicate previous studies**. Exact replication is hard to achieve, but repeating someone else's research design can add to your field by validating or refuting the initial findings. However, some committees frown on replicated research for theses/dissertations.

- **Adapt previous studies**. Some studies are conducted in a highly specific environment. Adapting a study to find out whether the findings can be applied to a new situation contributes to your field.

- **Expand previous studies**. The results from one study can spark multiple new questions that researchers did not know to ask. Researching one of these avenues broadens the base of knowledge for that topic and leads to new questions.

Problem complexity

Theses and dissertations are more complex than any paper you have written thus far in your coursework. Both are documents that contribute new insight into their associated disciplines. Thesis-level problems are less complex than those for dissertations, which also makes them shorter. Theses investigate elegant, yet simple, interactions between a limited number of factors. Dissertations, on the other hand, investigate complex interactions between a broader set of factors, which leads to conclusions broader in scope. It takes practice to develop the appropriate level for the appropriate document, which is why your adviser is so critical in the development of your research problem.

Current research problems within your topic

In the previous chapter, you prepared a list of topics and began building a network. Using the sources and contacts you made during that process, make a list of research problems within your topic that are currently being explored by others. Make special note of:

- Faculty research in your department
- Graduate student research in your department
- Other questions from conferences and seminars you attended

Best sources of potential research problems

Review the sources pertaining to your topic that you found while making the list above and working through the "Best sources of potential topics" section in the previous chapter. Toward the end of each article or written interview notes, look for phrases like "future studies may" or "with further research." Make a list of the scenarios associated with these phrases that seem interesting to you. Please note that the time it takes from choice to launch varies depending on where you found each item on that list. The following sources of research problems are listed in order of speed to start:

1. Faculty members with ongoing projects
2. Recently completed theses/dissertations in your topic
3. Future-study suggestions from conferences and seminars
4. Future-study suggestions from the literature

Your research problem

Rank the list you made above in order of preference and feasibility. Then, find an appropriate faculty member to agree to be your adviser. See the "Choosing an adviser" section in this chapter. Once those two things are done, schedule a meeting with your adviser and work with him or her to settle on a specific problem. For some, this process takes one meeting. For others, this takes a series of meetings. However it works out for you, it is important to be flexible and listen to your adviser with an open mind. Show initiative, but do not push. Show confidence, but steer clear of arrogance. Above all, once you come to an agreement as to what your research problem is, do not second guess it and open the discussion back up. Run with it.

LITERATURE: LEARNING MORE ABOUT YOUR TOPIC

In the course of choosing your topic, you have already become familiar with various types of information included in the broad term "the literature." You have identified the leading journals for your topic and figured out how to access them. You have even set up a system for recording sources as you find them. It is now time to develop a deeper knowledge of your topic.

Leading researchers

It is not difficult to figure out who the leading researchers are. A quick glance through the bibliographies of the studies you have already read will clue you in. Anyone who has three or more studies cited in the same article is a leader. Other methods for determining leaders are noting authors who come up three or more times when you type your topic into the library's search database, as well as those slated for keynote addresses at academic conferences.

However, just because someone is a leading researcher in your field does not mean you must agree with everything he or she finds. It does mean you will have to work diligently and accurately if you intend to pursue a research problem that conflicts with his or her findings. You will also need to become extremely familiar with this person's studies, to the point that you can discuss the strengths and weaknesses of them.

Effective applications of studies

Even if you lean toward a basic approach to your research rather than an applied one, all research findings are used in some form eventually. If you interviewed people from local agencies, review your notes and think about the research that must have preceded their procedures and successes. If you did not do any interviews, read through two recent studies on your topic and ask yourself:

- What are the implications of this study?
- How might the findings of this study be used to make a difference?
- Was the investment of time and resources worth the outcome?

There are no right or wrong answers to these questions. They are meant as subjective glimpses into your internal research perspective preference. However, it is important to understand your preference so you are working with it rather than against it as you develop your research problem with your adviser.

CASE STUDY: RESEARCH YOUR
TOPIC THOROUGHLY FOR BEST
RESULTS

Christopher Allen
Self-employed English teacher, editor, and writer
www.imustbeoff.blogspot.com

BIOGRAPHY:

Christopher Allen, a native Tennessean, teaches English in Germany. His writing has appeared online at *Metazen*, *Every Day Fiction*, and *BootsnAll Travel*, among others. In print, his stories have been anthologized in *Chicken Soup for the Soul* and *Gathering: Writers of Williamson County*, among others. He edits the literary e-zine *Metazen* and writes about his travels at **www.imustbeoff.blogspot.com**.

THESIS TITLE AND SYNOPSIS:

Henry James's Typology of the Empty Male: A Bakhtinian Discourse Analysis of In the Cage *and* The Golden Bowl.

In James's prose, there is a man characterized as imaginatively impotent: a "blank" man dependent on the feminine imagination to illuminate his own. Although critics have noticed this man in James's fiction, none has analyzed exactly how James executes this discursive sculpture. This thesis dissects Jamesian discourse through the lens of dialogic theory to elucidate what is found to be a primary aspect of James's late style: bland, absent, or impenetrable physicality. The empty male.

FIRST-PERSON ACCOUNT:

I encountered writer's block during the preparation and writing of my thesis. I was obsessed with writing a publishable thesis. I brooded over every sentence until the day my thesis director, with her dry sense of humor, said, 'Chris, just write the thesis. It's not like anyone's going to read it.' Far from being discouraging, her humorous outburst freed me. That day, a ton of bricks fell from my shoulders, and afterward, I believe my writing was more engaging.

My thesis director also inspired my interest in James. We had many general discussions of the author, but the idea of applying masculine gender theory combined with Bakhtinian discourse analysis to James was my own. My thesis director was supportive during the research phase, but I never felt she was doing more than her job required.

I have one tip for graduate students about how to write a successful thesis/dissertation: You don't have to write your thesis in one day. Enjoy the research. Experiment. Don't be afraid to write sloppy at first. As long as you have done your research thoroughly, you will work out a pleasing structure later. Meet your deadlines.

ASSISTANCE: CHOOSING AN ADVISER

If you joined any graduate student groups while working through the last chapter, you will want to connect with some of the experienced graduate students from these groups as you work through the next section. Their insight can be a valuable asset when deciding on which faculty member to approach about being your adviser first. Share your list of candidates, and ask what their personal experiences have been. Ask how many advisees each person is currently working with. Find out if the candidates are on time to appointments and focused on the task at hand during these appointments. Be respectful, especially if someone declines to answer, and keep these conversations confidential. You are all developing your professional networks; do not let your need for counsel jeopardize someone else's career.

As stated earlier, the development of your topic into a research problem and the selection of committee members are guided and overseen by your adviser. Because your research problem will drive your thesis/dissertation, it is important that your adviser be a productive member of the faculty with whom you can develop a positive working relationship. Friendship is not required, though it may develop. The point is to find a person who will teach you how to conduct research, both formal and informal, throughout your career.

Productivity

Your adviser's productivity is an important predictor of how smoothly your thesis/dissertation process will go. The best advisers publish regularly but not excessively. They might serve on an administrative committee but not so many committees that they are always in meetings. They might even serve as a peer reviewer for an academic journal or a low-level committee member for a professional organization. The key is to find someone involved with the professional community you are joining yet not too busy to give you quality guidance. Take the time to find out how your candidates measure up on these criteria.

Working relationship

As with any working relationship, effort should be expended on both sides. You are responsible for finding and reading sources related to your research problem, while your adviser is responsible for making sure you interpret those sources appropriately. You are responsible for scheduling and preparing for periodic meetings to discuss your research, while your adviser is responsible for attending those meetings with a focused mind. You are responsible for doing all the tasks required for completion of your thesis/dissertation, while your adviser is responsible for giving you insight into how you should complete those tasks. Through it all, trust should develop, so when it comes time to defend your work, your adviser has confidence in your abilities, and you have confidence your adviser will back you up.

Tenure considerations

Whether you are working on your thesis or dissertation, the process will take years. This means you need an adviser who will be around for years. Although life does take unexpected turns, there is one major predictor of your adviser's likelihood of being around for you from start to finish: tenure. Tenure equals job security; once attained, university employment is extremely difficult to lose. Before settling on your top choice, find out if that faculty member is tenured or just tenure-track. If this person is tenure-track, it means he or she is still trying to earn tenure. This will impact the way he or she functions as your adviser when it comes to negotiating on your behalf with other committee members and the administration. A tenure-track adviser may concede more easily — not because it is in the best interest of the research but because he or she wants to maintain team-player status among the tenured faculty. A tenure-track adviser is more likely to move on to a position at another university, especially if he or she feels that tenure is unlikely in the current setting. It is not impossible to complete a thesis or dissertation with a long-distance adviser, but it does add an extra layer of difficulty.

CHOOSING A COMMITTEE

Your committee will probably be your first introduction to the peer-review process. Universities require multi-person committees to sign off on theses and dissertations to be sure degree candidates have fully met the requirements. In a court of law, having multiple witnesses attest to the same facts lends credibility to testimony and facilitates a trustworthy verdict; so, too, with your committee. If three to five members of the faculty attest to the fact that you are able to participate in the academic discussion surrounding your topic, the university can grant your diploma with confidence. Viewing your committee as a quality-control board rather than a prosecutorial tribunal will greatly enhance your ability to navigate their requirements.

Support

Committee members, including your adviser who serves as chair, are there to support the acquisition of your degree. Supporting it does not mean blindly approving everything you propose or write, though. A truly supportive committee will thoughtfully weigh proposals and conclusions, flagging weaknesses when they see them. By doing this, they ensure your research and your writing will be the strongest they can be, thus supporting your overall career. Although you do want to avoid bringing on committee members who frequently lay down ultimatums, do not avoid potential committee members because you have heard they put challenging questions to students during meetings. The best support committee members can give you is a honing of your skills.

Relationship with the committee

Your adviser will have suggestions about who should serve on your committee. Take these under consideration carefully. Although all faculty members should be able to take an objective stance concerning your research and conduct themselves professionally, inviting someone onto your committee with whom your adviser has a known personal problem is asking for unnecessary trouble. Every committee meeting is bound to have its tense moments; there is no committee makeup that will avoid conflict altogether. What you want to avoid is a predictably flammable mix.

Conversely, if you develop personal problems with your adviser, it is best not to play your other committee members against him or her. Schedule an appointment with your adviser to try to work these problems out. If that does not work, seek advice from your department's graduate adviser.

Content gaps

Although your adviser will be an expert in one facet of your topic, he or she will probably not have expertise in every area necessary to complete your research. To ameliorate this, advisers often suggest choosing committee members based on gaps in their expertise. Depending on your research problem, one or more of your committee members may even come from outside your department. Develop the most well-rounded committee you can so you can benefit from the widest range of experience possible.

DATA: COMMON COLLECTION METHODS

By this point, you have completed your department's statistics course and become familiar with basic statistical principles. Remember that you are not expected to be an expert at this stage. But, you are expected to orient yourself to common approaches of analyzing the kinds of data your topic typically generates. Surveying the frequency of your topic being treated with a quantitative versus qualitative approach is a great way to start. Another is discovering whether your preference for basic versus applied approaches is in concert with the approaches taken in the literature. While you are surveying some preliminary studies according to these two criteria, start a tally based on the following data-collection methods and types of analysis. This will give you a good idea of the kinds of data-related tasks you will be expected to perform.

Data-collection instruments

During the design phase of your thesis/dissertation, you will be expected to develop data-collection instruments such as forms, surveys, or tally sheets. The instruments you develop will flow from the data-collection method you choose, which in turn flow from your research problem. Depending on the complexity of your research problem, you may use one or more of the following data-collection methods. Please note that the following methods are basic categories. Your discipline may have more specifically defined methods, but they should fit within these categories. Before reading further, pull out a stack of journal articles you have recently acquired or read. As you work through this section, you will develop a feel for methods that are common and uncommon for your topic.

Test

Tests measure performance of pre-defined variables. Variables can be anything perceivable with the five senses. Size, physiological reaction, and knowledge are common variables measured by tests. Standardized tests measure variables in study subjects and compare the results to a nationwide pool of anonymous subjects to gauge performance. Experiments measure test variables before and after a treatment to gauge performance.

Interview

Interviews record the verbal responses of study subjects to pre-defined questions. The responses may be recorded via video, audio, or notes. Interviewers may be remotely or intimately involved with study subjects. Interviewees may be randomly assigned or not; questions may be open-ended or tightly controlled. Conducting interviews is time intensive, but the details gained by complete and clarified responses are necessary for certain types of research problems.

Questionnaire

Questionnaires record the written responses of study subjects to pre-defined questions. Questionnaires are more impersonal than interviews and result in shorter answers. But, because gathering data via questionnaire is less time intensive, data sets are often larger — meaning more people gave answers.

Observation

Observations require a researcher to watch study subjects and record what they are doing and/or saying. Observations are commonly used in human and animal behavior studies, as well as background studies on topics for which the literature is scant. This method can be quite time intensive but often yields a great level of detail.

Content analysis

Content analysis asks a question and then searches existing literature and other sources that suggest an answer to the question. Content analyses often take a qualitative approach, but taking a quantitative approach is possible with the assignment of keywords and a scoring system to treat statements made about those keywords. Content analysis is a common approach to take in the social sciences.

BASIC TYPES OF ANALYSIS

Data without analysis is just a collection of information. Analysis is the process that allows researchers to find patterns, make comparisons, and draw conclusions about that information. The following section will walk you through a similar process to the one in the data-collection methods section, giving you a good feel for the types of analyses that are frequently used in your topic. Because detailed statistical instruction is beyond the scope of this book, make sure to have your statistics book or notes handy as you work through this section.

Central tendency

Measures of central tendency are descriptive statistics that generate an average value for a particular variable, which allows a pool of data to be represented by a single number. Common measures of central tendency are mean, median, and mode. Find a study in your stack that uses one of these measures, and answer the following questions:

- Under what categories were the study subjects grouped?

- Were traits within these categories ranked (ordinal data) or unranked (nominal)?
- Is the data categorized by pre-determined intervals?
- Is the data recorded on a relative scale (ratio)?
- How were these measures visually represented (graphs and/or tables)?

Variance

Measures of variance are descriptive statistics that quantify the amount of difference individual data points have from the mean of those points, in regard to a single variable. Common measures of variance are range and standard deviation. Find a study in your stack that uses one of these measures, and answer the following questions:

- Was there a large variance or small variance among the data?
- How is this variance reported?
- How is this variance visually represented (graphs and/or tables)?

Correlation

Measures of correlation are descriptive statistics that quantify the likelihood that two variables are related. Common measures of correlation are product-moment (Pearson's r), which looks at the relationship between two variables that were measured on an interval or ratio scale, and rank-difference (Spearman's rho), which looks at the relationship between two variables that were measured on a rank scale. Find a study in your stack that uses one of these measures, and answer the following questions:

- Which two variables were compared?
- Was there a strong correlation, weak correlation, or no correlation between the variables?
- Did the result line up with the researchers initial predictions?

Repeated measures

Repeated measures are descriptive statistics that quantify the state of a variable in a particular study subject across regular time intervals. Pre-subject data can then be collected into pre-assigned groups for analysis.

Find a study in your stack that followed variables over time, and answer the following questions:

- Over how many intervals was the variable measured?
- What was the attrition rate (loss of subjects over time)?
- How were the subjects grouped?
- How were the repeated measures analyzed?
- How were the repeated measures visually represented (graphs and/ or tables)?

Multivariate analysis

Multivariate analyses are inferential statistics that look for variance or correlation between multiple variables, with the added burden of predicting whether the results are applicable beyond the study groups. Common types of multivariate analysis are:

- MANOVA (multivariate analysis of variance), which compares the differences between multiple means of multiple variables.
- MANCOVA (multivariate analysis of covariance), which compares the differences between multiple groups across multiple variables.
- Multivariate correlational studies, which look for relationships between multiple variables.

Find a study in your stack that used one of these methods, and answer the following questions:

- Which variables were included in the analysis?
- Identify the dependent and independent variables.
- How were the results reported in the text?
- How were the results reported visually?

Statistical significance

Tests of significance are inferential statistics that predict the likelihood that differences found in descriptive statistics are true differences. Common tests of significance are:

- T-test, which compares the differences between two means
- Chi-square, which compares an actual sample to a hypothetical random sample
- ANOVA (analysis of variance), which compares the differences between multiple means
- ANCOVA (analysis of covariance), which compares the differences between groups

Find a study in your stack that used one of these methods, and answer the following questions:

- What kind of test was used?
- What kind of score was reported (t, chi-square, F)?
- How many degrees of freedom were reported?
- Which level of confidence was used?
- Did the researchers mention any effects they think sample size had?

Finding a data consultant

The best committees have someone whose strength is statistics. When your data consultant is a committee person, the help is free and available with an appointment. If no one on your committee is a statistical genius, your adviser should have recommendations of on-campus experts. Chances are your adviser has consulted with another faculty member for his/her own research. This does not mean your committee is weak in the area of experimental design. It just means that when it comes to statistical troubleshooting, you will need extra help.

There are also off-campus data consultants. They can assist you with planning and troubleshooting the collection and analysis of your data for a fee. A quick search online for "data consultant dissertation" will call up a list of agencies. If you add your location to the search, the list should narrow down to those near you. Make sure you search for reviews on the consultants you find and ask for testimonials from previous clients before signing any contracts. Ask other graduate students for recommendations as well.

If you do use an outside service, make it clear you need tutoring and assistance with your statistics. Allowing someone else to actually run the analysis for you will distance you from the process, potentially hurting you during your defense. You will be asked the what and the why about your design, its implementation, the analysis of results, and your interpretation of those results. Too much distance will make it difficult for you to answer these inevitable why questions.

Collecting data for others

Assisting other graduate students in their data-collection efforts will be one of the best data-related uses of your time in these early days of your journey. Beyond the gratitude and mentoring you can receive, you will get a glimpse into what will be expected of you. Like a "try before you buy" promotion for the latest home-improvement gadget, trying various data-collection methods before you settle on your own will give you an idea of your aptitude and preferences. If you do end up using one of the methods you tried, your time spent on someone else's project will be like on-the-job training. That kind of confidence and competence will give you problem-solving insight so your own data collection runs more smoothly.

WRITTEN WORK: DEVELOPING A MENTAL IMAGE

Even though you are not yet ready to begin writing your thesis/dissertation, you are ready to begin conceptualizing the shape of it. In order to spot counterfeit currency, the U.S. Secret Service recommends that you compare the bill you just received to one you know is genuine, focusing on differences rather than similarities. That is similar to what you will do in the following exercise — develop a mental image of what your document should look like and later recognize when yours does not match.

Read two recent theses/dissertations

Reading recent theses/dissertations from your department was suggested in the last chapter. In case you have not done that yet, consider doing it now. Any of these scholarly works available in your university's archives are successful examples of the kind of work you are gearing up to produce. But, to be most effective, you will want to use the following selection criteria:

- The same type of work you are planning to write (thesis versus dissertation)
- Completed within the last ten years
- Focused on your chosen topic or at least a related topic
- Overseen by your adviser or at least one of your committee members

As stated before, copies of theses and dissertations from your department's alumni are archived in your university's library. They may be archived in paper or electronic media but will be available for you to access either way. In your library's online catalog, search "thesis" or "dissertation," along with keywords from your topic. Click on the most relevant search results to confirm the work is from your department and completed recently. If it is marked as available, visit the circulation desk to check out a copy. If it is marked as unavailable but it is the perfect source, ask a librarian when and/ or how you may obtain a copy. You may not be able to see which faculty members were involved in a particular work until you can look inside at the acknowledgements, but do the best you can.

Build a thesis/dissertation model

Once you acquire two scholarly works to model yours after, read them both. Thesis and dissertation writing is different from other genres. According to Irene L. Clark, author of *Writing the Successful Thesis and Dissertation: Entering the Conversation*, students need an understanding of what a thesis/ dissertation is expected to do, look like, and be in order to successfully write one. Because you will not take a course specifically designed to teach the elements of this genre to you, take notes as you read your selected examples. Detailed analysis is not required here; jot down anything that stands out to you. Other factors to note are:

- Language elements, such as diction, sentence structure, and tone.
- Length of sentences, paragraphs, chapters, and the overall document.

- Organization of content, sections and chapters, graphs and tables, and citations.
- Style and font of text, quotations, section headings, chapter headings, bibliography, captions, table of contents, and title page.

These notes may be written out in longhand, typed bullet lists, or any other form that works for you. The important thing is to get multiple copies of these notes stored in your organizational system so you will have them at every stage of the writing process.

ORGANIZATION: IS YOUR SYSTEM WORKING?

Pull out the organization and recovery plans you developed in Chapter 1. How are you doing? Are your data stored in at least two places? Is everything neatly filed? Here is a test: Time yourself while you find one of the letters of introduction you sent out in preparation for interviewing local experts.

Did you find it in fewer than 45 seconds? If so, fantastic job. If not, spend some time filing and/or getting copies of your information into your back up system before you move on to Chapter 3. Hopefully, your system for tracking important dates is current because you are about to add some more.

UNIVERSITY DEADLINES

Missed deadlines are a massive threat to a successful defense of your thesis/ dissertation. Not knowing about a deadline does not excuse you from missing it, so now is the time to orient yourself to all the administrative deadlines you will be expected to meet. Get the latest copy of the graduate school catalog, which should be available from the university website. Make sure to add the file or URL to your organization system; paper copies may be available from the graduate school office. Skim through the major sections of the catalog, especially the calendar section, general requirements section, and the section pertaining to the college your department belongs to. Make a list of the following requirements:

- Number of units required for oral exam
- Number of units required per semester to keep process current ("continuous enrollment")
- Requirements for removing restrictions on an academic record ("encumbrances")
- Time frame for demonstrating proficiencies and removing deficiencies
- Maximum time from enrollment to graduation
- Graduation application and fee
- Scheduling requirements for proposal and defense
- Filing requirements for final thesis/dissertation version

Once you think you have a complete list, show it to an experienced graduate student and your adviser to ensure you have not missed anything. Add these dates to your organization system. Then, on a piece of graph paper, make a timeline that starts with your admission to graduate school and ends with your expected graduation date. Add tick-marks to the line in evenly spaced intervals, with one tick-mark per semester (there are typically three semesters per year). Add color-coded notations for the deadlines as they pertain to you, and mark your current location on the timeline. Save this visual and update it once a semester to remind yourself how far you have come and to keep the finish line in your sights.

SUMMARY OF TASKS

Phase 1

- Choose your topic.
- List potential research problems within your topic.
- Decide if you prefer basic or applied research approaches.
- Obtain an adviser.
- Collect data for others.
- Build a thesis/dissertation model.

Phase 2

- Finalize your research problem.
- Determine leading researchers for your topic.
- Obtain a committee.
- Survey common data-collection and analysis methods for your topic.
- Find a data consultant.
- List the university deadlines involved with your thesis/dissertation.
- Tidy up your organization and disaster-recovery systems.

Chapter 3: Read

You have your topic. You have your adviser and committee. You even have your research problem. Congratulations — you have entered the reading phase. Now, make sure you do not get mired in it. Reading can be a bit like quicksand: The more you do, the farther you sink. This chapter will help you read enough to design your study, write your literature review, and knowledgeably discuss your topic without losing yourself in tangential literature.

TOPIC: REVISION

If you develop a habit of filtering your reading choices through your research problem, you will avoid casting too wide a net in your survey of the literature. Reading academic sources takes a lot of time and energy. But, if you are working and/or caring for a family, you do not have much time and energy to spare. It is easy to be led by others on what you should read, and it can be almost too simple to let your curiosity take you from one study to the next. Resist these urges by asking, "How does this study relate to my problem?" If the answer is weak or nonexistent, leave the source in the stacks to read another year.

As you read, you may find your research problem needs revision. This revision should merely be a honing of your problem, not a complete overhaul. Major changes to your research problem may result in delays because of extra reading or new methodology requirements. New studies are published monthly, sometimes with exciting implications. Resist the urge to substantially alter the research problem that may have taken you and your adviser hours — or even weeks — to settle on. Instead, jot the idea down in your organizational system as a potential future project.

LITERATURE: REASSESS YOUR SELECTION

As a review, the term "literature" in this sense spans a full range of academic sources. Books, journal articles, professional conference proceedings, interviews, case studies, seminar notes, and even documentary audio-visual productions are included in this category. Your role in the literature review is not to passively read as much of these sources as possible. Active engagement with the literature is required for this phase to be functional. This means absorbing the information, picking out portions useful to you, and thinking critically about whether the sources truly accomplish what they set out to. The ultimate goal of your literature review is to validate the purpose and design of your planned research. Read to reach it.

Focused selection of sources

The scope of literature brought to your attention by using only your topic as a search term in your library catalog will result in too much information for you to process and use. Selecting a list of keywords and using Boolean logic will help you narrow this search. Boolean searches use basic mathematical logic expressed in words (such as "and" for additions, "or" for subtractions, and "not" for divisions) to refine the results of a keyword search. For instance, in a Boolean search through the NIU library's catalog, the topic "competition" displays 5,841 results. By using the Boolean search term "and" with a keyword added, like "competition and plants," you can knock the results down to 19 sources. An even more complex Boolean search for "competition and plants not invasive" trims the results to 17 sources.

Somewhere in these narrowed results will be an applicable study whose bibliography will point you to more applicable studies. Reading through the abstracts or summaries of these sources will give you clues as to whether they are worthy of your time. Look for philosophies, study subjects, methodologies, and research aims that might be appropriate guides for your research problem. Although a few might not give you the information you hoped for, you will have already saved yourself valuable time by weeding out other more obviously unrelated studies.

Productive reading

Productive reading means spending time with appropriate literature — time that moves you forward in your thesis/dissertation process through improved comprehension, methodological awareness, and/or scholarly diction. Productivity is enhanced by focused selection of sources, reading at the right time of day, reading in the right location, and reading on the right media. "Right" is a subjective measurement based on your personal preferences. For example, e-book enthusiasts would be best served downloading as many sources in .pdf format as possible and reading them on their favorite devices, while paper enthusiasts would be better served reading photocopied sources.

It will take a bit of practice to ensure forward movement from your time spent reading. In written form, assess your productivity after reading the first 25 focused sources you access using the following list:

- Source number *(See the "Sources" section of Chapter 1)*
- Time it took to read
- Time of day read
- Reading location
- Media type
- Associated keywords
- Most applicable things learned through reading

Once you have done this 25 times, you may notice patterns. If you find some studies leave you grasping for an answer to "most applicable things learned," ask yourself why you chose to read those studies. This may lead you to develop better search strategies that exclude this type of study in the future. If your decision to select these studies seems valid, then see if there is a pattern between time of day, reading location, or media type and your difficulty in finding ways to apply the study to your thesis/dissertation. Use these patterns to your advantage, reading well-selected sources in the most optimal conditions possible.

Note taking

Even if you have a photographic memory, note taking is imperative during the reading phase. Memorization or familiarity with sources is not enough. You will need to record your process of critically thinking about each source, including which portions you plan to implement in your own study and why. Depending on the organizational system you have developed, these notes may be electronic, paper, or a combination of the two. No matter how you chose to organize your notes, you will be able to find and cite these sources during the writing phase if you have assigned each source a number, as suggested in Chapter 1.

Taking notes on the following items will ensure you get what you need from each source within one or two passes. This does not mean you will not revisit sources, but it will mean you can quickly decide which source to revisit and actually find it. Before taking your notes in earnest, scan the "Data" section of this chapter so you may accomplish all your note-taking tasks for each source over the course of the same read. *See Appendix A for a sample note-taking form.*

- Source number
- Complete bibliographic data, especially authors, title, and year
- Exact wording of the research problem
- Major results and conclusions (just enough to be a memory aid)
- Key points that apply to your research problem

- Your reaction to those points (questions, doubts, application to your own research problem)
- Quotations with exact wording and page number
- Notable items from the writing style (diction, sentence structure, paragraph length)
- Notable items from the methodology; see the "Data" section on the following pages
- Keywords the study should be filed under

Through the course of preparing your proposal, you may end up using spreadsheets or tallies to better use portions of this information. If you penciled more notes on a paper copy of the study or embedded notes in an e-version, make sure to note that somewhere on your note-taking form. A simple asterisk with "more notes at [location]" will suffice

CASE STUDY: STICK TO THE SCHEDULE

Dr. Mary Crowe
Director, Office of Undergraduate
Research, the University of North
Carolina at Greensboro
mcroweuncg@gmail.com
www.uncg.edu/our

BIOGRAPHY:

Dr. Mary Crowe is the director of the Office of Undergraduate Research at the University of North Carolina at Greensboro, a position she has held since spring 2006. She has extensive experience in mentoring university students on projects related to the behavioral ecology of invertebrates. She likes to involve students in her research on dung beetles. Prior to her current position, she was the Director of Xavier University of Louisiana's Center for Undergraduate Research from June 2004 to January 2006. From 1994 to 2004, she was a tenure-track/tenured faculty member in the Department of Biology at Coastal Carolina University (CCU). While at CCU, she mentored the research projects of 30 students in the field of crab foraging and thermoregulatory behavior. More than one-third of her undergraduate students have gone on to obtain their master's and doctorate degrees, and she has served on multiple master's thesis committees. Dr. Crowe earned her bachelor's in Biology from Eureka College in 1987, then her master's and doctorate in Biology from Northern Illinois University in 1990 and 1994, respectively.

DISSERTATION TITLE AND SYNOPSIS:

Larvae Aggregations in the Imported Willow Leaf Beetle: Mechanisms of Reaggregation and Adaptive Significance

The work focused on two different questions related to aggregations of a beetle: "how" and "why." We found the beetle larvae cue in to secretions from each other (much like caterpillars do) to find their way to each other and new leaves to feed on. The group size of the species varied to just a few to more than 16. There appeared to be selection for middle-sized groups: If the group was too small, the larvae could not puncture the leaf to establish a feeding site; yet if the group was too big, it could attract more predators than a smaller group.

FIRST-PERSON ACCOUNT:

I earned my degrees (master's and doctorate) in the catalog-estimated time period. I think my doctoral adviser was pivotal in helping me navigate the process, encouraging me to break my dissertation up into pieces. Based on her input, the first chapter of my dissertation was a review and in press (accepted for publication) while I worked on the other chapters. I was able to separate the other experiments into sections and worked on one section at a time. I would start on the next section while waiting for the reviews of the previous section so there was a continuous process of writing, editing, and rewriting. One strategy I used — and continue to use to this day — is to set artificial and accelerated deadlines for myself and work hard to treat those deadlines as seriously as those imposed by my adviser and theses/dissertations committees.

The skills above have absolutely affected my ability to publish and earn tenure. I believe another skill, listening, was just as important. Every year, I underwent an annual review where I met with the department chair and dean to ascertain my progress toward tenure. I listened closely to their evaluation of my progress and where I needed to center my energies in the upcoming year. For example, in year two, I was told I was fine in getting external support for my work but really needed to get some publications in the pipeline. I had already lined up student researchers for that summer, but the following academic year I did not work with any students and concentrated on writing up publications.

When I serve as an adviser, I do notice a transformation of my advisees' organizational habits and their development as researchers, though I think the improved organizational skills come sooner than some other research skills (improving a person's writing skills takes a longer time). I do not specifically talk to advisees about organizational skills and time management, but I find leading by example seems to work. Pulling up a calendar and charting out the tasks with students helps keep us all organized. We share a Google calendar, and students can see notices for draft one of a given manuscript, including notes/appointments I keep for myself. We place meetings on the calendar for when drafts of introductions and abstracts are due as reminders. When a new student joins the group, we have a short overview meeting in which everyone talks about the lab's research policy.

I have one tip for graduate students about how to write a successful thesis/dissertation: Schedule writing during the time you are most productive on your calendar — at least every other day. I am best first thing in the morning, and I use that time to write. Mid-afternoon, my brain is dead. I use that time to exercise or run errands, never to write. Even if you get writer's block during that specified time, do not leave your computer. Do something — anything related to the writing of your dissertation, such as working on an outline of a subsequent chapter or the summary of a manuscript, anything that will eventually contribute to your work.

ASSISTANCE: UTILIZING YOUR HOURS

For the most part, you will be on your own during the reading phase. No one can do the reading for you; however, all current graduate students are required to register for thesis/dissertation hours, even if they are not taking coursework. Make sure to take advantage of your registration for these hours by checking in with your adviser periodically and attending seminars. These on-campus visits will give you opportunities to maintain your peer network with the other graduate students. At no point along your process should you become a ghost.

Present key sources to adviser

Pardon the pun, but it is imperative to stay on the same page as your adviser during the read phase. Make periodic appointments with him or her to discuss key studies you feel have major implications for your own research. Keep each appointment focused on one source and supply your adviser with a copy in whichever medium he or she prefers to read. Spending the time and effort to discuss these studies will keep your reading productive because it:

- Keeps you visible, which improves adviser confidence in your abilities and effort.
- Allows you to get feedback on your ability to appropriately cull information from sources.
- Allows your adviser to suggest on-point studies you may not have found.
- Allows your adviser to suggest new people to consult.
- Keeps your adviser apprised of the direction your research is taking, allowing for course corrections if necessary — before you have blown too much time.

The last thing you want is to present your first draft of a literature summary only to have your adviser call your interpretations into question and negate the usefulness of the bulk of your reading. Periodic consultations, scheduled at your adviser's convenience, should prevent this kind of time-intensive surprise.

Attend departmental seminars

At first glance, departmental seminars seem like optional events. But, taking the time out from reading and other obligations to attend will help you develop critical-thinking skills. It is not essential for you to be the one raising your hand asking questions. What is essential is to listen to the presentation, think about the visual display of information, and analyze the appropriateness of the conclusions drawn. Even if you are just in "sponge mode," absorbing information without being able to analyze it, you will be able to learn from the analytic ability of others in the room. What points are they calling into question? How and when are they expressing their questions? How does the presenter respond?

If the seminar presenter was brought in from another institution, the sponsoring faculty member might hold a reception for the presenter. Check to make sure your attendance would be appropriate. If so, these informal gatherings would be an excellent place to let the presenter know you are new to the topic and to ask some questions you may have been too embarrassed to ask during the formal seminar. This is a good way to broaden your network and demonstrate enthusiasm for the research process.

DATA: METHODOLOGIES TO UTILIZE

During the read stage, collect as much information as you can about the methodologies other researchers have used to investigate your topic and how you might apply these same methodologies. By focusing your energy on methodologies in your literature rather than the vast number of methodologies that exist, it will be possible to dig in and eventually understand the "why" behind them. Understanding the why will help you select the one most appropriate to your problem and defend that choice.

Survey common methodologies for your topic

The "Sample note-taking form" mentioned in the "Literature" section simply lists "notable items from the methodology." *See Appendix A for this sample.* Discomfort with statistics may make reading the data and analysis sections of articles difficult. The following series of questions will walk you through these challenging yet vital portions of the literature so you know which kinds of information to list in your notes.

Research type

- Which research perspective was used?
- Which research type was used?
- Do the authors give reasons why? If so, list the main ones.

Data collection

- Which data-collection method was used?
- What kinds of data-collection instruments were used, and who developed them?
- Did anything go awry with the collection of data?

Data analysis

- Which descriptive statistics were used? Why?
- Which inferential statistics were used? Why?
- If something went wrong during the data-collection phase, what did the authors do to deal with it?
- How did the authors visually represent these findings? Did their chosen method work for you?

Rationale for the researchers' choices

- Do the authors seem excessively preoccupied with justifying their methodological choices? Why do you think that is?
- Does the rationale align with your statistics book's explanation of when and how their choices were made?

- Do you think the authors made the best choice? If not, what would you have chosen? This is an intricate line of questioning; do not be alarmed if you cannot answer this when you first start reading.

Your access to similar methods

Keep practical matters in mind as you survey appropriate methodologies for your research problem. If you are working on a thesis, do not begin planning your research around a method that took another researcher five years to complete. If you are a single mother of toddlers, you should probably pass on a methodology that requires extended, out-of-town data collection. But, access can be dependent upon more than personal constraints. Some methodologies require expensive equipment your university may not have. Unless you can find another facility with the necessary equipment and a sponsor who will make sure you get time with that equipment, look for alternative methods. Some groups of study subjects, especially children, are difficult to gain access to unless you already have some connection to them. If these groups are critical to your research problem, you may have to be flexible and creative in working through barriers to access, such as privacy concerns.

Consider carefully how much effort you want to expend in gaining access to elements of your methodology. Doing an informal cost-benefit analysis before you settle on something complex will ensure the amount of time and energy you put into this area will be worth what you get out of it. To do a quick and dirty cost-benefit analysis, ask yourself the following questions using a scale of 0 (none/nothing) to 10 (a lot):

1. How much money will this methodology cost?

2. How much time will this methodology cost?

3. How much frustration and stress will this methodology cost?

4. Add up the answers from questions 1-3.

5. Do I have access to people that can reduce the frustration/ stress factor? If so, by how much can they reduce it?

6. How applicable is this methodology to my specific research question?

7.   How many difficulties will I encounter if I end up using a different methodology?

8.   Add up the answers from questions 5-7.

Subtract the answer in number 4 from the answer in number 8. If the result is positive, then you may have good reason to pursue the methodology. If the result is negative, you may want to start searching for alternatives. This little exercise is just that — a quick exercise to help you think about your choices. Ultimately, your decision will have to be based on discussions with your adviser.

WRITTEN WORK: DOCUMENTING YOUR RESEARCH

Even though there is no written work to turn in for a grade during the reading phase, there is writing to do. Taking notes, drafting outlines, recording questions and insights all are important documents you will generate as you read the literature. If crafted diligently, they will be of great assistance during the actual writing of your proposal. There is no right or wrong way to draft these documents. Prepare them in whichever format on whichever medium will be convenient and conducive to study.

Notes

In the sample note-taking form, it mentions "keywords the study should be filed under." Assigning keywords to sources is a terrific way to group them for easy reference during the design and writing stages. In order to access any source you need any time you need it, make lists for each keyword on paper or in a spreadsheet:

- The keyword is the header for the list.
- Column 1 is the source number.
- Column 2 is the location of the source in your regular system.
- Column 3 is the location of the source in your disaster-recovery system.

- Create a fourth column, which will be used later to assign a chapter of your thesis/dissertation in which the source will be used.

If you create these lists on paper, make duplicate copies, and file them alphabetically in a keyword folder or tab in your system. If you use spreadsheet software to record the lists, save the file as "keywords," and create separate sheets for each keyword. That way you can easily flip back and forth using tabs when a single source belongs to multiple keywords.

Outlines

You may want to outline sources of particular interest. Creating an outline from the text will give you a detailed look at its construction, logic, and flow of ideas from question to conclusions. This is a time-consuming exercise, so choose the sources with care. By this point in your research, you will have a feel for which sources are the most important to absorb. Store these outlines with the sources in your system for later reference.

Questions

As you read, you will have questions: questions about why and how the authors conducted their research the way they did, questions about whether or not an author's conclusions were supported by the evidence given, or just plain questions because you do not understand something. Record all these questions, along with the source number they pertain to. Seek out more experienced graduate students, your adviser, or some other trusted mind to discuss them. If the questions are short ones pertaining to a limited section of a source, you might be able to e-mail one of your mentors to ask the question along with the wording of the section. If the answers you seek are long and involved, set up a meeting in advance, and provide a copy of the source. If appropriate, offer to treat your mentor to an off-campus snack to make the discussion more enjoyable and show how much you value your mentor's time and assistance.

Your thoughts and reactions

There is a space on the "Sample note-taking form" for your thoughts and reactions to statements made in your sources. Taking care to record these as you read will help you develop your research problem and write your literature review thoroughly. You will be reading so many sources that you will forget these thoughts if you do not write them down. The last thing you want to do is reread all your sources at every stage of your thesis/dissertation. Even worse would be to decide not to make a point in your writing because you cannot find the source that prompted it.

ORGANIZATION: STORE EVERYTHING

Throughout the reading phase, you have encountered a few new sources of information to track. Keep your paper versus electronic preferences in mind as you decide where to store quotations and records of logistics. Both types of information have a funny way of disappearing in the heat of the writing phase.

Quotations

As with the keyword lists you made in the previous section, making a quotation list will help you access the quotes you are looking for when you are looking for them. Your quotations should be listed under the most appropriate keyword in the same medium you chose for the keyword lists you developed earlier. The format is as follows:

- A keyword is the header for the list.
- Column 1 is the source number.
- Column 2 is the first ten words of the quotation.
- Column 3 is the location of the source in your regular system.
- Column 4 is the location of your notes on the source.
- Create a fifth column, which will be used later to assign a chapter of your thesis in which the quotation will be used.

File your quotation lists alphabetically by keyword, as with your keyword lists; paper versions alphabetically in folders/tabs or electronic versions in alphabetically arranged sheets. Using the source number and location information, you will quickly find either the original source to confirm wording or the notes on the source to review your thoughts on the quote.

Recordkeeping

In Chapter 1, you chose a place to record important dates. Is this location able to track the logistics surrounding those dates? For meetings, develop a way to organize maps and directions, parking information, and preparatory notes. For deadlines, develop a way to store and access instructions and expectations related to the tasks. For research trips, develop a system for tracking expenses such as photocopying, mileage, and meals. Review the organization section of Chapter 1 to remind yourself of electronic and paper methods at your disposal.

Maintenance

With the copious notes and sources you have generated during this stage, it is vital you tidy up. During your journey through the literature, you may have run across some sources that did not fit any of the categories you set up in Chapter 1. Take the time now to classify them, duplicate them, and store them in a logical place within your system. Make sure your organizational and disaster-recovery systems are up to date before moving on to the design stage.

SUMMARY OF TASKS

Phase I
- Hone your research problem.
- Select a list of keywords.
- Assess your reading productivity.
- Select well-focused sources.

- Attend departmental seminars.
- Outline two or three sources of particular interest.

Phase 2

- Take detailed notes from your sources.
- Discuss sources with your adviser.
- Survey common methodologies for your topic.
- Make keyword lists.
- Make quotation lists.
- Discuss your questions regarding the literature with mentors.
- Include logistics in your organization and disaster-recovery systems.

Chapter 4: Design

Once you have read enough to be familiar with the literature pertaining to your research problem, you are ready to enter the design phase. This chapter will help you design your research and will prepare you for writing your proposal, beginning with the most appropriate format for the written statement of your problem. Keywords helped you stay focused during the Read stage; in the Design stage, you will keep yourself and your committee focused by choosing, highlighting, and repeatedly using key sources in addition to keywords. Productive conversations with your adviser and committee will contribute to the successful devising of the actual methodology for your study, which includes choice of data-collection method, choice of research location, and a provisional time frame for completion.

TOPIC: TYING UP LOOSE ENDS

After completing the Read stage, you have developed some expertise within your topic. You may have worked hands on with some facet of it while you explored which area to focus on. You and your adviser have even come to an agreement on the specific research problem your thesis/dissertation will address. As far as topic goes, the hardest part is now behind you. There are still some communicative loose ends to tidy up like the official statement of your problem and a list of guiding questions to keep you focused, but these tasks will take less time and effort than the initial development of your problem.

Choosing the most appropriate way to state your research problem

How you word the research problem in your thesis/dissertation depends on more than what sounds good or the use of proper grammar. Although clarity of thought is important, there are logical and statistical considerations as well. Outside the realm of mathematical and physical laws, proving that a statement is true within 100-percent certainty is not possible. What is possible is finding data to support the likelihood that a statement is true. Even easier is finding data to support the likelihood that a statement is false. The tactic you choose to take will affect the format of your research problem statement.

Hypothesis

A hypothesis is a research problem written as a statement of prediction. After combining personal experience with background literature, researchers have enough of a feel for their topic to make predictions that have a reasonable chance of being supported by data. The hypothesis includes a statement of a given situation or trait plus a prediction of how that situation or trait is affected by a given factor. Hypotheses must be precise and specific to be useful because your methodology must include strategies for exploring enough of its angles to draw robust conclusions.

This prediction process is not unlike predictions in everyday life. Past experience serves as an informal review of the literature that gives insight into the interactions between words, situations, and people. For instance, you might know your mother-in-law will be highly upset if your family will not visit her at Thanksgiving. However, based on past experience, you have found she is frequently mollified by receiving bad news in the form of a detailed handwritten letter on floral stationery. You predict she will refrain from nagging your spouse to change plans if you write the news, complete with explanation, on the violet-trimmed paper she gave you for your birthday.

Depending on the type of analysis method you choose, you may need to reword your hypothesis as a null hypothesis during the analysis stage. A null hypothesis states a prediction that there will be no effect of the factor on the variable in question. During the analysis phase, you will attempt to disprove the null hypothesis which, like a double-negative, supports your actual prediction. In the previous example, the null hypothesis would be that the notification method will have no effect on your mother-in-law's choice whether or not to nag your spouse to change plans.

Question

A question is a research problem written in the form of, you guessed it, a question. It asks what effect a factor will have on a situation or trait without making predictions that need support or refutation. This type of research problem has the tendency to be open ended. Although this leads to the ability to include unexpected findings in your analysis, be sure it is not so open ended that your committee can keep adding more and more queries to your project. The more specific you make the question, the more focused your methodology will be, thus making your research manageable. In the previous example, the research problem written as a question would be, "What effect will writing on violet-trimmed paper have on my mother-in-law's reaction to our plans not to visit at Thanksgiving?"

WRITING YOUR QUESTION OR HYPOTHESIS

You may choose to work through this section now or wait until you have worked through more of Chapter 4. The official statement of your research question will need to be fluid until you and your committee have completely approved your methodology. You may even work through the following questions multiple times during the Design stage. By the time you finish this chapter, you should have the finalized statement of your research problem, which will be included in your proposal. Ask yourself the following:

1. What was the overall question that led to my research problem?

2. After extensively reading the literature on the topic, what do I think the answer is?

3. How large is this overall question?

4. Do I need to limit or broaden its scope? If so, what classifications and qualifications can I use to do that?

5. Do my analysis options require the use of a null hypothesis?

6. Which form is used most often in my topic: hypothesis or question?

7. Which form is most appropriate for my research problem: hypothesis or question?

8. How will I word the statement of my research problem in my proposal?

DEVISING GUIDING QUESTIONS TO KEEP YOU FOCUSED

Within any given research problem are a string of smaller questions that encompass the multiple facets of information needed. Developing a series of guiding questions that walk you through the logical steps needed to gather and analyze the information necessary to treat the research problem will prevent you from getting sidetracked along the way. It will also make it more difficult to add extra data-collection exercises that might unnecessarily complicate your analysis. While devising these guiding questions, you may find you have forgotten to take various data needs into consideration while devising your main hypothesis/question. Now would be an excellent time to discuss this with your adviser and make any needed revisions. Be sure these guiding questions restrict themselves to the scope of your research problem instead of expanding into new territory.

Use keywords

In Chapter 3, you developed a set of keywords to focus your literature research. You will now use them to focus your research methodology. Pull this list out now and review it. If any of the keywords ended up leading to information you have decided not to use in your research problem, write a small x next to them so you know to disregard them while you work. Choose the most important and independent five keywords from your list as starting points, and organize the rest of your keywords by their relationship to those five. Relationships should be visually represented in a way that works for you; for instance, as an outline or cluster diagram. To make a chart of your research's logic that incorporates your keywords:

1. Select a large piece of clean paper. A whiteboard may be substituted if you prefer.

2. Draw a centered arrow the length of the paper's longest side. If you prefer to work in landscape orientation, draw the arrow from left to right. If you prefer to work in portrait orientation, draw the arrow from top to bottom.

3. At the start point of your arrow, write the overall question that led to your research — as stated in the "Writing your question/hypothesis" section.

4. At the end point of your arrow, write the statement of your research problem.

5. Add the five main keywords at points along one side of the arrow in an order that makes logical sense for the progression of thought needed to get from the question at the start point to the research problem at the end point.

6.   For each keyword, write a question that incorporates the concepts you will need to investigate or analyze in order to successfully investigate your research problem. Use related keywords to make these questions as specific as possible. These are your guiding questions.

Drive the project

With your guiding questions in hand, you will be able to drive your project with clarity and focus. Whether you are presented with a new research article or a suggestion to add a new form of data collection, you will be able to run these requests through your guiding questions and decide whether they are appropriate ways to spend your time and energy. You will then be able to back up that decision if asked with on-point wording and objective reasoning. The last thing you want is for a committee member to suggest you investigate a new facet of your topic, and you refuse with nothing more than a reason, such as, "It will take too much time," for your refusal. These guiding questions will also keep your own curiosity in check. Keep the chart in a highly accessible location within your organizational system.

CASE STUDY: IT ALL COMES DOWN TO YOUR ADVISER

Alan W. Graustein
Retired from the Position of
Northeast Regional Director
Association of Christian Schools
International
alan_graustein@acsi.org
www.acsi.org

BIOGRAPHY:

Dr. Alan Graustein worked in public and private schools as a teacher and administrator before joining the Association of Christian Schools International (ACSI). He worked as a Regional Director for ACSI, which involved working with Christian schools to obtain and retain accreditation, as well as organizing conventions along the northern half of the eastern seaboard. Now retired, he still serves as a consultant part time.

DISSERTATION TITLE AND SYNOPSIS:

Increasing Membership in the Northeast Region of ACSI

This work identified advantages of membership and systematically applied specific marketing strategies over a one-year period. The methodology involved produced an increase in membership of more than 10 percent.

FIRST-PERSON ACCOUNT:

I earned my degree from a highly organized low-residency program. This structure enabled me to conduct my applied research project while "on the job." My day-to-day experiences provided an opportunity to identify the problem and to consistently implement solution strategies.

My college adviser was most helpful while trying to design my research, and the marketing research done by Dr. Philip Kotler proved invaluable. It took three years to earn my degree, which was considered "on-time." The greatest help for me was a system of "deadlines" implemented by my adviser. I had just enough flexibility in my work schedule to free up the required time at critical points in the project.

> If I could give one tip to graduate students about how to write a successful thesis/dissertation, it would be to identify a faculty adviser who is highly skilled, demanding, yet fair. Then, keep the lines of communication open without becoming a pest.

LITERATURE: STRENGTHENING YOUR SUCCESS

Even though you are finished with the bulk of your reading, you will need to continually review and refer to the literature you have amassed. If you have taken detailed notes and stored them in your organizational system, this review will be no trouble. Remember that the literature you have read is not only the foundation of your research but also the justification for it. Knowing your sources will strengthen your position in discussions with your committee and others crucial in the successful completion of your research.

Identify key sources

How many sources have you read so far? If the answer is hundreds, it is not surprising. It is also too high a number to keep the salient points ready to mind at all times. Part of this problem is dealt with by the keyword list you made in Chapter 3, which includes the sources that pertain to each. With this list, finding an appropriate source to answer the question at hand is mere minutes away. There will be some sources you refer to repeatedly because they are foundational to your research and use methods that will be best for your own project. Designate these as key sources, and study them frequently.

If you are having difficulty deciding which sources are your key sources, use the following criteria:

- You accessed the source ten or more times while developing your research problem.

- Your research problem developed as a direct result of the content of the source.
- Your research subjects are extremely similar to the subjects in the source.
- Your methodology will most likely be similar to the methodology in the source.
- The source used a visual representation of data you may likely use.
- The source is referred to in ten or more of your other sources.

You may develop other criteria more specific to your research problem. Add these criteria to the list above, and use them to designate all your key sources. Once you have a complete list, make sure to review your notes on these sources once a week, as well as rereading these sources once a month. The better you know them, the less time you will have to spend looking them up when their information is needed.

Identify other supporting sources

If you identify sources that specifically support your research aims and methodology, you will be able to readily separate the background from the problem-specific sources in your notes. Taking the time to do this now will simplify the writing of your literature review later. Both background sources and supporting sources are important and worthy of a place in your literature review. Supporting sources will be more frequently referenced during discussions with your adviser and committee. It will also be important to demonstrate that statements made in your key sources have support from other researchers. This kind of support makes everyone involved with your research more confident that its premises are valid and will result in a worthwhile addition to the discipline.

To decide which sources are your supporting sources, take out the notes for one of your key sources and:

1. On a clean sheet of paper, write the authors and title of the key source across the top of the paper.

2. Make two columns, one labeled "support" and the other labeled "conflict."

3. Review the "key points that apply to your research problem" from your original note sheet.

4. Jot down any authors or studies that come to mind whose studies related to these points.

5. Use your keyword lists to find the notes for those studies.

6. Review the notes for these studies. If a study supports your key source, write the authors and title in the "support" column. If a study refutes or otherwise conflicts with your key source, write the authors and title in the "conflict" column.

7. For the studies that conflict, spend some time thinking about the differences in findings. Are there flaws in the conflicting study's methodology? Were there circumstances that do not apply to your research? Are there ideological differences between the study's authors and the key source's authors?

Although you will spend more time reviewing the supporting sources, it is important to prepare ahead of time for challenges your committee may approach you with regarding the conflicting sources. Just remember that academia thrives on debate. Being able to calmly and precisely communicate your side of a conceptual conflict is a skill that graduate school should help you obtain. It is hard to support your methodological choices if you have not previously thought through other researchers' choices and why they are not the most applicable to your situation.

ASSISTANCE: CREATING A ROUTINE

Proper guidance and assistance are vital to the successful navigation of the Design stage. Many considerations must be brought into research design;

someone new to the field cannot possibly manage them all without help. Fortunately, you do not have to design your research on your own. Once a faculty member accepts a role as your adviser or committee member, he or she has a duty to help you. But, it is your duty to help these busy faculty members do their duty by making it as convenient, efficient, and enjoyable for them as possible.

Periodic meetings with adviser and committee members

Establishing routine meetings with your adviser and committee members may seem like a time-consuming plan. It may even seem to you like it would be an imposition on the faculty members in question. But, periodic meetings scheduled at regular intervals will make things convenient, efficient, and enjoyable in the long run by:

- Adding an element of familiarity to the relationship you have with your adviser and committee, minimizing the mystery and fear that accompany proposal and defense meetings.
- Demonstrating your diligence and determination.
- Eliminating your adviser's need to check up on you.
- Keeping your adviser and committee apprised of developments so you do not have to spend proposal or defense time getting them oriented.
- Allowing your adviser and committee to highlight areas of concern or propose course corrections before you have spent a lot of time pursuing problematic items.
- Providing frequent opportunities to diffuse or prevent conflict because of misunderstandings.

If you must prioritize your time, spend the bulk of your meeting time with your adviser. He or she will be the most critical to your successful completion and defense. The frequency of these adviser meetings will depend on your situation. For the hard sciences, students often receive desk space in their advisers' labs. In this case, it would not be unusual to have weekly informal meetings with advisers. In disciplines where the majority of graduate students are part time while working in the profession, such as education or social science, monthly meetings may make more sense because of logistical concerns. If meetings must be spaced a month or more apart, make sure to keep in touch with small questions or discoveries via e-mail on a regular basis.

In the Read stage, you met with your adviser to discuss studies you had recently read. You might have even discussed whether a particular study might be applied to your own research. The discussions of the literature during the Design stage, however, should focus on to *how* to apply particular studies to your research, such as sample data-collection techniques, appropriate analysis methods, or descriptions of problems you will need to avoid. These will be in-depth discussions, not of the article as a whole, but of the particular kernel of insight you will be gleaning.

As far as meetings with committee members go, it will be up to you and your adviser whether you meet with the committee as a whole prior to your proposal. However, during the Design stage, you may run across questions neither of you can answer. If these questions fall within the expertise of a committee member, find a way to meet with him or her. If your adviser suggests you meet with the committee member, you are all set and may make the appointment with confidence. If not, mention the following to your adviser (via e-mail or in person) prior to the appointment:

- You plan to meet with the committee member to discuss the question.
- You would like to know if your adviser has any other questions he or she thinks you should ask while you are there.
- The date range you are hoping to meet with the committee person.

Giving prior notice will give your adviser confidence you are keeping things moving by accessing appropriate help. It will also give your adviser the opportunity to let you know if he or she has a problem with the proposed meeting before you have involved the committee member. You should be able to meet with your committee members without a lot of drama, but odd things do happen within a department from time to time. Personality conflicts between faculty members, competition between faculty members for an administrative position, or even unfounded gossip can impact your adviser's wish to bring a particular committee member onto his or her "home turf" (i.e. your research). It is better to keep out of the mix whenever possible.

Seminar attendance

In the Read stage, you were encouraged to attend departmental seminars to observe standard operating procedure for presentations. Continue to attend (or start if you have not already), paying special attention to the methodology section of the presentation. This will give you a great opportunity to practice what you have learned by reading the literature and taking your department's statistics course. Try to analyze the presenter's choice of:

- **Study groups**: What characteristics did the study groups have? How did the researcher gain access to the groups? Were the groups diverse/focused enough?

- **Sample size**: How large were the sample groups? How was this size determined? Was it adequate?

- **Data-collection instruments and procedures**: How was the data collected? Were any problems reported? Would this work for your data collection?

- **Analysis methods**: Which methods were used? Why? Do you see any problems with that choice? Would any of these methods work for your situation?

- **Conclusions**: Do you think the conclusions are supported by the data? Why, or why not?

Taking notes during the presentation in this way will make your attendance active rather than passive. Try to ask a question each time you attend. Raising your hand in a room full of faculty and experienced graduate students may be intimidating, but it will give you practice speaking in front of a group so you are not as nervous during your proposal and defense.

CONSULTANTS

If you have chosen to use the services of consultants outside your committee, the Design stage is a critical time to contact them. Before using any billable hours, however, make sure to run your use of consultants past your adviser. There are legitimate uses of consultants, such as devising complex data-collection instruments or setting up a database to house your data, but you need to make sure the tasks you outsource are not tasks you are supposed to be learning to do on your own.

When signing up for consulting services, make sure to read all the fine print. Know what services are and are not included in the fees you will pay. If not already written in the contract or description of services, get a promise in writing that the consultant will explain the what, why, and how of everything produced for you. The last thing you want is to stand in front of your committee during your proposal and not know the answer to questions about your methodology.

Timing is an important consideration prior to and during your use of consultants. The use of consultants should facilitate your journey through your thesis/dissertation by making it faster and/or easier. Hire a consultant who can meet with you on your schedule and furnish results on time. If you must meet with the consultant on his or her schedule, you may run into delays if you are unable to communicate your needs in a timely fashion. Late completion of services for any reason will frustrate you and your adviser and negate your reason for contracting the tasks out in the first place.

PARTICIPANTS

If you are pursuing a degree in the social sciences, education, psychology, or other fields that use humans as study subjects, you may be planning research that involves people as data sources. In the United States, this kind of research is governed by the Office for Human Research Protections (OHRP), a division of the U.S. Department of Health and Human Services. According to the OHRP website (**www.hhs.gov/ohrp**), their mission is to give "leadership in the protection of the rights, welfare, and well-being of subjects involved in research conducted or supported by the U.S. Department of Health and Human Services (HHS)." This includes privacy protection, protocols for respecting subjects and guarding their dignity, and safeguards against conflict of interest. If you visit the OHRP website, you may feel intimidated at first by the seemingly endless number of links to resources, guidelines, and oversight procedures. Fortunately, you do not have to navigate their system alone.

Your university should have an Institutional Review Board (IRB) that will assist you in the approval process of the portions of your methodology that involve human participants. Take a moment to look for the IRB on your university's website. It should state which data-collection methods are classified as research, such as questionnaires, surveys, interviews, tests, observations, and other experimental procedures. Look for their definition of "human subject," based on data-collection type, such as interactions, interventions, and personal information. Make sure to browse their links to university-wide forms and guidelines, and ask your adviser if there are additional department-specific forms.

Northern Illinois University (NIU), for example, requests that researchers fill out a screening form prior to filing an actual application. This screening form, available as a download from their website (**www.orc.niu.edu/orc/human_research/index.shtml**), gets turned in to an Authorized Departmental Reviewer who is trained to assist the IRB in forwarding on only those studies that need their protocol approval. Their checklist of conditions may rule a methodology out of its domain if it utilizes:

- Deceased human subjects
- A methodology that does not fit the IRB definition of research

- Nonpublic dissemination of results
- Public sources of data

NIU uses criteria set by the OHRP, so the previous conditions will most likely apply to your university's IRB process as well.

Your adviser should be able to tell you when to start the IRB process. You may not need to start it until after your proposal has been approved, but you will facilitate the design of your methodology if you are already taking these requirements under consideration. Please note that if your research involves animals rather than humans, your university should have a similar process to go through to ensure the animals are treated humanely. Again, your adviser should be able to point you in the right direction.

Sources of participants

Getting approval to use human research participants is not the only hurdle your methodology faces. Finding humans willing to be your research participants will be a challenge unto itself. If you are already working in your field, say as a teacher or therapist, you may already have access to participants. However, if you do not have a study group already at hand, you will have to be creative and determined. Start your search with any supportive local experts you found during the Prepare stage, and move on to any other local groups that may have members who would be a good fit. Churches, schools, clubs, and hobby groups are all possibilities. As you continue your search for participants, presentation of yourself and your research problem will be of paramount importance. How you present yourself to potential participants depends on the age of the participants and the level of intrusiveness your data collection will require.

If you are researching a problem involving children, you will first have to pitch your project to gatekeepers (parents, teachers, counselors). These gatekeepers take their responsibilities regarding children's welfare seriously. They will be looking for someone honest, professional, and engaging who can communicate the research goal in everyday language and answer questions with patience and grace. If you come across as impatient or cannot make yourself understood, you will not be trusted with their precious charges. You must also understand that these gatekeepers may have had difficulties in the past with participation in research. A study may have imposed on too much time or published results that painted an unflattering portrait of a given situation. Listen carefully to the concerns these gatekeepers communicate to you. If they bring up something major you had not thought about yet, let them know you will take it under consideration, and ask if you may present a revised version of the project later. Handing out some kind of pamphlet or information sheet will show you are prepared and organized — two well-respected traits in someone who wants to interact with children. Above all, do not try to exert any kind of pressure or sales technique. Your project will either be a good fit or a bad fit. The more convincing you have to do at the beginning, the less likely you are to develop the lasting trust and confidence needed to collect your data effectively.

If you are researching a problem involving adults, you will most likely pitch your project directly to potential participants. The formality of your pitch will depend on its aims and intrusiveness. A casual survey in which no personal, identifying information is collected may be pitched in an informal manner; for instance, addressing a whole group while wearing jeans. An experiment in which there is physical intervention, for instance a blood draw or environmental manipulation, should be pitched in a formal manner one-on-one while wearing dress-casual clothing or possibly a lab coat. The same communicative principles in the previous paragraph apply to this situation, but you will have more opportunity to respond to and connect with your potential participants. Beware, though, of revising your methodology based on the concerns of any one individual. If you hear the same concerns from a majority of your participant pool, you probably want to revise your protocol. If just one person has a problem, it is probably best that he or she declines to participate. Again, prepare something in writing to hand out and be willing to give the person ample time to think about participating if possible. Please note that if your adult-focused research involves mentally disabled adults, you might need to pitch your project to their guardians first because of patient-protection protocols of the organization/facility serving them.

Intrinsic benefits to participants

The concept of basic versus applied research was introduced during the Prepare stage. By now, you will have determined which approach your research problem takes. Why does this matter when talking about participants? It matters because more people will agree to help you if your research intrinsically benefits them. Intrinsic benefits are positive things a person gains by doing a task, such as knowledge, enjoyment, or feelings of self-worth. People are self-motivated when completing intrinsically beneficial tasks, which facilitate the collection of high-quality data from them. Applied research inherently seeks to do something helpful with its results so it will be easier for people to understand how they might experience benefits from participating.

This is not to say that a basic approach does not contain the possibility of providing intrinsic benefits to participants, just that the link is a little harder to make. Give this some thought before you make your first pitch if you are using a basic research approach. Will the conclusions you draw from your research lay the groundwork for applied studies later? What kind of applied studies might be possible after you have conducted your research? Do not twist anything or link your research problem to something far-fetched. Some research problems will only ever be for the joy of knowing. If this is the case, go with it. During your pitch, make sure to show a passion for your topic so your participants can connect with it through your excitement. Who knows, you may get them so interested in your topic that they want to participate purely out of curiosity.

Methodologies that involve play of some sort are also intrinsically beneficial. Developing a data-collection instrument that feels more like a game than a test will help participants engage. Enjoyable interaction with objects or people can add an element of play. Even something as small as adding comfortable objects or images to the environment where the data is collected can help people feel like they are "playing hooky" from their usual duties.

There are research projects that offer extrinsic benefits to participants, especially those that involve extensive intervention. Extrinsic benefits are rewards and privileges a person earns by doing a task, such as a stick of gum, a $20 gift card, or meeting a celebrity. People are externally motivated when completing extrinsically beneficial tasks, which make them more likely to slack if their effort no longer seems worth the reward. If this happens, you may need to promise more and more in order to obtain a complete data set from a given participant. Extrinsic benefits usually cost money — money you will not have unless you have obtained a grant — so it is probably best to stick to developing intrinsic benefits for participants.

DATA: THINK THROUGH YOUR DESIGN

Before working through this section, make sure any methodological notes you have taken are handy. If you took a departmental statistics course, get your textbook or course notes out as well. If you are still not comfortable with common methodologies used in your discipline, take the time to review the concepts introduced in the Data section of this book's previous chapters along with the notes you took while working through those chapters. The section you are about to read will focus on helping you think through the design of your own methodology rather than continuing with data-related instruction.

Time period and complexity

When working with your adviser to design your methodology, the possibilities seem endless at first. However, there are real administrative constraints to the time you have to complete your thesis/dissertation, which in turn constrain the complexity of your methodology. Even though you most likely have economic and personal constraints as well, administrative constraints will be a better bargaining chip when negotiating limits to your methodology with your adviser. The time limitations discussed below may be used as a general guide but may vary widely by discipline. Check your graduate school catalog to see how much time the school estimates this should take and the maximum allotted time you have to complete your degree.

Thesis requirements

A thesis tied to the pursuit of a master's degree is meant to introduce the candidate to the research process, including learning to communicate with the academic community. Completion of the thesis makes the author eligible to teach at the university level but with limits. For instance, it does not permit the author to act as an adviser to doctoral candidates. The complexity of a thesis-level problem should be greater than an undergraduate project paper but less than a dissertation. The preparation and writing of it should teach the author the basics of selecting a topic, collating background literature into a cohesive foundation, and researching in such a way that a small contribution is made to the topic. Ultimately, the size and scope of thesis-level research should be such that it can reasonably be completed within the administratively allotted time.

The amount of time a thesis should take to write varies depending on whether the author is a part-time or full-time student. Regardless of enrollment status, though, students must complete the required coursework and thesis within six years. Coursework alone can take one year full time or more than three years part time, but a good rule of thumb is your thesis should take the same amount of time to complete as your coursework. If you are working on your thesis full time, you should design a methodology in which data collection can be completed in six months to a year. If you are working on your thesis part time, you still want to design a methodology in which data collection can be completed in six months to a year because it could take you two years to complete the literature review, analysis, and writing of your thesis.

Dissertation requirements

A dissertation tied to the pursuit of a doctoral degree is meant to develop the candidate into a full-fledged academic peer. Completion of the dissertation makes the author eligible to teach at the university level without constraints, including the ability to act as an adviser when the time is right. The complexity of a dissertation-level problem should include multiple factors that require a great deal of analysis to treat. The preparation and writing of it should establish the author as an expert on the topic and equip the author with the skills to conduct research independently in the future. Even though this level of mastery and complexity will take a much longer time than a thesis, it still has an administratively limited time. Extensions are sometimes granted, but eventually, time runs out.

The amount of time a dissertation should take to write varies depending on whether the author is a part-time or full-time student. Either way, though, students must complete the required coursework and thesis within nine years. Coursework alone can take two to three years full time or more than six years part time, but a good rule of thumb is your dissertation should take one-half to two-thirds of the time you are enrolled in graduate school. If you are working on your dissertation full time, you should design a methodology in which data collection can be completed in 18 months to three years — this estimate varies widely by discipline. If you are working on your dissertation part time, use this same time estimate for data collection, and allow for the entire dissertation-writing process to take up to six years.

Your research perspective

Up to this point, you have been introduced to the concept of qualitative versus quantitative approaches to research, as well as identifying which perspective the bulk of the literature on your topic takes. If you are still a little shaky on the difference, review the definitions of qualitative and quantitative research in Chapter 1 or in the Glossary, and practice making the distinction in the most recent ten journal articles you have read.

Once your memory is refreshed, work through the following questions to determine which research perspective your thesis/dissertation will use:

1. Will the bulk of my data be in the form of extended written response or samples from available literature?

2. Will the bulk of my data be in the form of numerical values?

3. Does my research problem assume a subjective view of reality in which perception plays a key role?

4. Does my research problem assume an objective view of reality in which measurements play a key role?

If you answered "yes" to numbers 1 and 3 but "no" to numbers 2 and 4, then your research perspective is qualitative. If your answers were the exact opposite, then your research perspective is quantitative. If you answered "yes" to any three questions, your research may incorporate a mixed perspective. Discuss this with your adviser to make sure it will not create any problems in your analysis later on.

Your research type

As a reminder, the main research types are descriptive, correlational, causal-comparative, experimental, and quasi-experimental. The time you spent during the Read stage figuring out which sources used which research types will help you play an active role in the decision of which type to use. This choice is a complex and time-consuming one. If you have developed a productive working relationship with your adviser, you can select the most appropriate research type together. If your adviser works in a more hands-off way and you use a consultant to walk you through this choice, make sure your adviser is kept apprised as things develop. Before discussing your research type with anyone in earnest, write down provisional answers to the following questions:

- Who/what is your ideal study subject? ("Subject" here refers to human participants, other living organisms, inorganic substances, or documents.)

- What are the characteristics your ideal subject should exhibit?
- What will be your primary source of data (survey of the literature, direct observation, measurements, etc.)?
- What format will your primary data be in (words, numbers, images, etc.)?

Once you decide on a research type, spend extra time studying how it is used within your topic. Review your key sources, study how they implemented elements from that research type, and think about how to implement them in your own.

Your data-collection method

The choice of your data-collection method will be intertwined with your choice of research type. Once you have chosen your primary source and form of data above, you can decide the appropriateness of collection via tests, interviews, questionnaires, observations, and/or content analysis. Working out all the details for data collection can take weeks, sometimes months, so exercise patience. Rushing the process can lead to weaknesses in your data because of preventable problems with data collection or collecting data that does not actually answer the questions you asked. On the other hand, getting mired in all the nuances of data collection can slow down — or even halt — progress on your thesis/dissertation. Aim for a balance between diligence and drive while working with your consultant and/or adviser to develop an effective data-collection method in a reasonable amount of time. Some of the details you will be planning are:

- Descriptions and characteristics of data to be collected
- Specific criteria for inclusion/exclusion of data from a given subject
- Intrinsic (and possibly extrinsic) benefits that live subjects will receive from participating, if applicable
- Frequency and duration of data collection
- Specific conditions the collection environment should meet

- Step-by-step description of the collection process, including storage of data after collection
- Pre-determined solutions to predictable problems

Developing your collection instrument

Part of your methodology will be the design of your actual data-collection instrument. This may be a highly specific note sheet, a survey, measurement table, or other document built to record the information you need for analysis. Make sure to design something that will be specific enough to keep your data collection focused and complete enough to prompt you to glean everything you need from a given subject. Consultants and advisers can be of great use during this task, but you should prepare for design discussions by thinking about:

- The format(s) your data will be in.
- Paper versus electronic instruments for capturing this type of data.
- The number of distinct data points that will be collected from each subject.
- The time needed to collect these data points and the feasibility of taking that much time.
- The effect that potential collection instruments might have on the data collected — if studying human participants.
- The differences in cost of potential collection instruments.
- Your physical ability to collect data via potential collection instruments.
- Whether others will use the collection instrument.

Once you have finalized the elements your instrument will contain, think about whether you have the skills to make a professional-looking version of it for presentation to your committee during the proposal. If you do not have strong graphical or word-processing skills, you may want to trade labor with another graduate student who does. Begin asking around so you will have the trade in place before moving on to the Propose stage.

Finding your research subjects

As stated in the "Research type" section, "subjects" in this discussion include human participants, living organisms, inorganic substances, and documents. Where you find your research subjects will depend on what type they are. For example, if you are gathering data from documents, you will look in a library or some other archival location. Obviously, this type of location will contain a vast number of documents, but not all are potential research subjects for you. Use the list of inclusion/exclusion criteria you previously developed to find documents that are eligible to serve as subjects for your research. Be strict with yourself. The more consistent you make this determination, the stronger your results will be.

Strict adherence to your inclusion/exclusion criteria will benefit you regardless of the kind of subject you study. If you have a lot of difficulty finding subjects that meet these criteria, you may have to go back and rethink the criteria. For your results and conclusions to be robust later on, however, make sure to do any revising of selection criteria before any data is gathered so no one can accuse you of skewing your research to make it fit your predictions.

For instance, if you were studying the difference in overall driving behavior on a winding rural road in a speed-trap zone versus outside a speed-trap zone, you might have made the prediction that people would drive faster outside the speed-trap zone than in it. However, as you collect your data, you notice — because of the snail's pace at which they drive by, thus allowing for identification — that elderly drivers and out-of-state drivers do not change their speed. Deciding mid-stream to exclude elderly and out-of-state drivers in the midst of your data collection for fear that your results will not turn out "right" is an example of data manipulation, which is forbidden. However, if you wanted to begin noting specific data points as "elderly" or "out-of-state," you could later run analyses on this subset of your data that look for differences between elderly, out-of-state, and other drivers. These additional analyses should be run *after* you have analyzed all the data according to your original methodology with all drivers included.

Your data analysis method

Another lengthy process you must walk through now is choosing one or more analysis methods to use on your data. Whether you are designing qualitative or quantitative methodology, at some point, you will have to gather all the data you have collected and analyze it. If you are working on a qualitative study, this analysis may be highlighting notable data points and looking for patterns. If you are working on a quantitative study, this analysis may involve using statistical formulae to determine the difference or similarity between traits. You definitely need assistance when determining which analysis methods to use on your data because each method carries assumptions about the data that must be met — assumptions that are complex and take experience to work through for a given data set.

Work closely with the person designated as your data consultant to make sure you consider the assumptions and limitations associated with various analytic procedures while you design your analysis. Make sure to bring a summary of your research type, research method, and data-collection methods with you during these discussions. If your data consultant is not your adviser, keep your adviser updated as the design of your analysis develops. You do not want to spend days or weeks working with (and potentially paying) a consultant developing an elegant analytic design only to have it scuttled by your adviser's disapproval.

Research location

The location(s) in which you collect your data should be carefully chosen based on suitability and logistics. Come up with a list of locations, including preferred and backup choices. Backup locations are important because the proposal process takes time, and things at a preferred location could change during that time. Other logistical constraints, such as changes in family or job responsibilities, can change during that time as well. Having a list of suitable backup locations will keep you from having an approved methodology but no place to carry it out.

Access

In order to guard against any misunderstandings or difficulties with accessing your research location once it is time to collect your data, get any necessary permissions documented in writing of some sort. Be it a library card for literature surveys or a signed letter from a site director for biological field research, having a tangible document stating you are allowed to be there doing what you are doing will prevent delays and frustration. In this age of increased vigilance and concern over safety and privacy, your presence could be questioned by security guards, receptionists, or even just concerned citizens passing by. You will be able to limit the number of questions and get on your way faster by having proof that you are legitimate. Sometimes this proof will require a lengthy wait for administrative processing so start pursuing this documentation now rather than waiting until after your proposal is approved.

Time and focus

The time it takes to travel to and from your research location can take time away from other tasks, be they duties to family, an assistantship, or an employer. If this travel time allows you to forget about the rest of the world and focus on your data collection, then choosing a location a reasonable distance away could be beneficial. On the other hand, if this travel time is fraught with frustration and stress, it may not be worth the time — especially if there is a reasonable alternative nearby. The last thing you want to do is arrive for your first data-collection session irritable and tired because that is when distraction and errors creep in. This is especially true when you collect observational data. Arriving to your research location in a focused and energetic state will also reduce the chances of forgetting something, either in preparation or follow-through, which will save you from spending additional time returning to correct errors and omissions.

Expense

Researching the feeding habits of Amazonian tree frogs in their native habitat by its nature will cost more money than researching the frogs' feeding habits in a local zoo. Nearly every topic can be studied in ways that involve exotic and not-so-exotic locales. The expense of travel, loss of paid work hours, and necessary equipment must all be considered when planning your research location. Unless you are independently wealthy or have acquired grant funds, you will need to conduct your research in a region near you.

Some graduate students find a location that requires a bit of a drive and an overnight stay actually makes their data collection more effective because they are free from everyday distractions. Others find the travel wearying, which makes their data collection less effective because mistakes and oversights get made. Do an informal cost-benefit analysis based on your personality, preferences, and the gains to be made from traveling during data collection. Will you have to rent or buy equipment at your research location in order to conduct your research? Will there be additional insurance costs? Will there be additional child-care costs associated with your absence? Be honest with yourself while doing your cost-benefit analysis, especially because things usually end up costing more than you anticipate.

Sample size

When it comes to sample size, you might think bigger is better. This is not always the case. Your sample size will be a function of your research perspective and type, your data-collection method, and your analysis method. For instance, if you conduct qualitative research with case studies, your sample size will need to be small or else your task will be an analytic nightmare too large to finish in your allotted time. Remember that "sample" in the term "sample size" refers to the fact there is a large pool of people/animals/things that fit your criteria, but you only collect data from a subset of it. The trick is finding a representative sample, in which the number of subjects and their overall characteristics allow you to generalize your findings to the pool as a whole. Before you talk to your data consultant about what sample size is right for your study, think about the following:

- There may be generalized guidelines in your discipline that suggest which sample size to use. These guidelines are based on the data-collection method and the size of the pool you sample. These guidelines may be referred to as heuristics.

- There may be model sample sizes from your literature review. What sizes do you find most often in studies that used a similar methodology to yours? What sample sizes did your key sources use, and why?

- There may be discipline-specific or analysis-specific formulae and tables for calculating sample size. Power analysis, one example, was developed to figure out the minimum sample size required to reach a specific level of statistical confidence. But, with some experiments, using the minimum sample size is not recommended. Ask your data consultant whether calculations of sample size in this manner are indicated.

No matter which sample size you end up using, it is important to know why you use it. Getting help and guidance when choosing a sample size is completely appropriate, but make sure you understand the range of choices you had and the reasoning behind the one you eventually chose. Not only will it prepare you for making similar choices in the future, but it will also help you defend your choice when presenting your proposal to your committee.

WRITTEN WORK: CORRESPONDENCE

Aside from any applications you may have to fill out, the written work in the Design stage is restricted to correspondence and personal notes. Correspondence with your adviser and committee will be in the form of e-mail. Be courteous and professional at all times, even when writing a casual reply. Read through every e-mail at least once before clicking "send" to make sure the tone and content are appropriate. And above all, be sure when replying to a message that your reply is solely going to the recipients you intend.

When corresponding with potential participants, you may use a similar technique to the one presented in the Prepare stage for approaching local experts. Show your respect for the participants' time by keeping the letter to one page, though you may enclose a pamphlet or information sheet if you have one. If you correspond with the leader of a group rather than many individuals, follow up after a week with a phone call or e-mail to see if the leader has any questions.

As far as personal notes go, write down everything possible: ideas that hit you while drinking coffee, seminar notes, meeting notes, your thoughts about sources you read, and your latest design iteration. Be sure to use keywords to track your notes. The notes you took during the Read stage will be used in your written proposal's Literature Review section; the notes you take during the Design stage will be used in the Proposed Methodology section. The more complete and organized your notes are now, the easier time you will have writing your formal proposal.

List of keywords and their definitions

In the Read stage, you made an extensive list of your keywords that included related studies. This document is vital, and it contains an enormous amount of information. Content you have absorbed while reading the sources pertaining to a particular keyword have shaped your perception of that keyword. However, your adviser and committee may not share that perception. In order to make sure you all speak the same "language" when using your keywords, create a glossary. This glossary should contain:

- An alphabetical listing of your keywords
- Your working definition of each keyword
- Bibliographic information for two key sources you read that helped you develop this definition

This glossary may be shared with your adviser as soon as you feel it is ready for inspection. Asking your adviser to review it will ensure you have appropriately interpreted the literature. It will also keep the two of you in sync. You may format the glossary in any manner that looks professional and orderly, but suggested formatting for each single-spaced entry is:

- Keyword on its own line, flush left, in lowercase, bold
- Working definition on the next line, entire definition indented five spaces, in standard punctuation, standard typeface
- Bibliographic information on the next line, bullet listed, to include authors, year, title of article/chapter, and title of journal/book
- Double space after each entry

Get your adviser's guidance as to when the best time would be to distribute the glossary to the rest of your committee. It may be best to save it for now and attach it to your written proposal later. This document at the very least will ensure you use these keywords consistently while writing your proposal and thesis/dissertation.

Notes from meetings and planning sessions

During the Design stage, it is important to keep every scrap of information generated during meetings that focused on the planning of your research. Even after you and your adviser have agreed on a methodology, things may change during your proposal once the rest of your committee gives additional input. If you have documentation tracing all the steps you took to develop your methodology, you can readily pinpoint the section troubling your committee and fine-tune. If you do not have this documentation, you may find yourself ripping out vast segments of your methodology and starting over because you cannot remember your original rationale.

Although you may have a keyword-based organizational system to store these notes long term, consider adding some kind of chronological breadcrumb trail for the meeting notes. This could be in the form of a dedicated meeting journal in which every entry is dated or merely a list of dates that includes the locations of pertinent notes. The term "notes" here is used broadly to include text, photographs, audio recordings, sketches, mind-maps, flow charts, and any other medium that records outward expressions of thought. If you work in a primarily digital workflow, the list of dates with file locations is probably your best bet. Keep this chronological list or journal readily available until your methodology is finalized and your data collection has begun.

ORGANIZATION: DATA

You may feel inundated with information to track at this point, but do not worry. It is all part of the process of learning what does and does not work for you in terms of organization. Take this opportunity to improve your ability to control the information you generate so you are able to manage all the data you collect. A successful defense depends on reliable data and its analysis. Missing data are a lot easier to explain to a committee when the loss is due to forces outside your control rather than a failure on your part.

Acquire departmental style guidelines

Because you will write your proposal once you complete everything in this chapter, it is time to get serious about style guidelines. You have already constructed a personal style guide based on the model theses/dissertations you found during the Explore stage. However, to successfully write an acceptable academic document, you will need more specific guidance than that. Because of methodological and philosophical differences between all the various academic disciplines, the official style guide you should use while writing your thesis/dissertation will vary according to your department. Using the NIU website as an example again, a simple search on the term "style guide" yields more than 20 pages of results. A quick scan through these results indicates that:

- The English department uses the Modern Language Association (MLA) style guide.
- The Mathematics department uses the American Psychological Association (APA) style guide.
- The Music department lets students decide which style guide to use.
- The Sociology department uses the American Sociological Association (ASA) style guide.

Find the search box on your university's website, and type in "style guide [department]." Skim through the results to find a document that definitively states which style guide your department prefers. If you cannot find a straight answer, write down the names of three style guides that are mentioned most often in the search results. Then, contact (via e-mail or in person) your adviser, and simply ask which one is his or her preferred style. Once you get your answer, decide how you will access it. Your university's library should have print copies, as well as an online access account. However, if you are a paper person and work best at midnight, you might want to invest in buying your own print copy. You should be able to find used copies for a reasonable price at Half.com® (**www.half.ebay.com**) or at Powell's (**www.powells.com**).

ORGANIZATION: AVOIDING DISASTER

Design notes, correspondence, applications for human or animal research, a keyword glossary — you have accumulated all this and more while working through this chapter. But, do you have it organized? Test yourself now by timing how long it takes you to access your notes from the most recent seminar you attended. Did it take you less than three minutes? If so, then reward yourself with a half hour of fun, and excuse yourself from reading the next two subsections. If not, then read on.

Your organizational system

Where did you eventually find your seminar notes? According to your organizational plan, where were you supposed to find them? How many other places did you look before you found them? The answers to these questions may be highlighting a flaw in your initial organizational design. The intent to be organized is never the problem. But, somewhere along the way, some kind of mental hiccup is interfering with your follow-through. These problems may stem from:

- New types of media you did not think you would use when you planned your system.

- New keywords that required an extensive reshuffling of your filing system because of alphabetical issues or lack of space.

- An internal dislike or discomfort with the primary source of media you chose to use (paper versus electronic).

- A complicated system that takes more effort and time to maintain than frantic, disorganized searches.

If any of these organizational stumbling blocks resonate with you, brainstorm ways to tweak your system that address the applicable issues. *Review the Organization section of Chapter 1 to look for options that may work better for you now that you know what kinds of media you are accumulating.* Take the time to make small changes to your system, and test them out by getting everything filed that needs it. However, if you are considering a complete overhaul of your system, resist. Your desire to spend time organizing all over again may be your subconscious attempt to avoid moving forward in the thesis/dissertation process.

Your data recovery plan

If you have trouble keeping your organizational system up to date, then you are probably not keeping up with your data recovery plan either. Before moving on to the Propose stage, take the time to make sure all your materials are safely backed up. Copy electronic files, and store them in appropriate folders. Upload files to your cloud-computing solutions. Make a trip to the photocopier and then to your fireproof safe. Whatever strategy you have planned for duplicating and storing your data in case of disaster, do it now. Once this is complete, evaluate your backup plan with the above criteria for your organizational system, and see if any minor changes can be made to lure you into backing things up more often.

SUMMARY OF TASKS

Phase 1

- Write the official statement of your research problem and guiding questions.
- Identify key and supporting sources.
- Identify inclusion/exclusion criteria for study subjects.
- Choose your research perspective and research type.
- Write a keyword glossary.
- Acquire a copy of the department-preferred style guide and sample proposals.

Phase 2

- Begin the search for study subjects and research location.
- Choose your data-collection method and design associated instruments.
- Choose your analysis method.
- Determine your target sample size.

Chapter 5: Propose

You have prepared yourself for research, explored your discipline until you found a topic, read through the literature to develop a research problem, and designed a methodology with which to study it. Now, it is time to prepare and defend an official proposal of your thesis/dissertation research. Depending on the degree you are pursuing and your departmental preferences, this process may be an informal affair between yourself and your adviser or it might be a presentation in front of your entire committee. Feel free to adapt the steps in this chapter to fit your situation. This chapter is written with the more formal process in mind of presenting and defending a proposal.

TOPIC: AMENDING WHEN NECESSARY

When you first prepared for your thesis/dissertation, you read in terms of a wider topic. Although you have successfully narrowed this topic into a specific research problem, some of the related yet off-point concepts you read will still float around your mind. Beware of the distracting potential of these concepts, even if a committee member brings them up. Committee members like to throw around additional possibilities because they do not necessarily know everything you have already considered. If one of these possibilities triggers a memory of something you read and you engage in conversation about it, you may end up having to amend your research problem to include it — an amendment that will add time and complexity to your research. The more focused you are on your specific problem, the easier it will be to say, "That is an interesting thought, possibly to research later, but I think it is outside the scope of the problem at hand."

WRITE YOUR TITLE

The seemingly obvious step of writing a title for the proposal document is frequently forgotten until the last minute. However, writing the title at the outset of the proposal process rather than the end allows you to synthesize everything you have read and outlined up to this point. It gives your brain thinking time in which to orient itself to the writing task. This orientation will set your subconscious working on ways to logically communicate the background to, support for, and elements of your proposed research which will make the rest of the writing flow faster from your conscious mind. How you word the title of your proposal will influence how you word the title of your actual thesis/dissertation, so spending quality time on this now will make things easier down the line.

Driven by your research problem

Your title should be driven by the research problem you have selected to study. Find the document that contains the official problem statement you wrote in the Design stage. Read through it several times, and highlight the key phrases from the problem statement. These phrases should serve as the basis of your title. For instance, if your problem statement was a hypothesis such as:

"In the home environment, use of the ignore technique coupled with a flat-affect verbal prompt labeling the technique will decrease the number of aggressive behaviors exhibited by highly verbal teens with high-functioning autism."

You would highlight the phrases:

- Home environment

- Ignore technique
- Flat-affect verbal prompt
- Decrease aggressive behaviors
- Teens with high-functioning autism

If you find yourself tempted to highlight the entire problem statement, do not. Look through the wording, and determine which parts are main concepts versus qualifiers that describe the main concepts. The qualifiers are important for narrowing the scope of your research, but they are not the best words to include in the title.

Include keywords

Keep this highlighted version of your problem statement out, and find the keyword glossary you built in the Design stage. Scan through the words you have highlighted, and look for words defined in your glossary. Underline these words, including words with the same root but in a different form, such as "aggression" rather than "aggressive." Most of the phrases you highlighted should contain at least one keyword. If most of the highlighted phrases do not, add keywords to your glossary that pertain to these phrases.

Additional tips

Successful proposals are those that have been approved and research has officially begun. If you can access successful proposals from other graduate students in your peer network, do it. If you cannot, ask your adviser for some proposals he or she has on file from previous graduate students. Writing titles requires a specific kind of voice. A quick scan through the titles of your peers' proposals will help you slip into the title voice more easily. Characteristics to pay attention to are length, verb tense, format, complexity of phrase, and whether the title is in a complete sentence or a sentence fragment. How closely do these sample proposal titles mirror the hypotheses/questions? Do they use the word "proposal" in the title or subtitle? Do they use any words pertaining to their methodologies? Getting permission to make a copy of a proposal will allow you to study it for the duration of your proposal writing.

After all this preparation, is your title ready to fly through your fingertips? If not, write your highlighted phrases as a centered list on a blank sheet of paper. Try to play an altered version of connect-the-dots, where the highlighted phrases are the dots and transitional words are the lines. If you cannot logically connect the phrase dots, try rearranging the phrases until you can. Eventually, you should be able to write a title that reads like the samples from your peers. Open up a word-processing document and type your title, your name, and any other identifying information in a style that mirrors your sample proposals. Insert a page break, and save the document under a file name that includes the word "proposal" in it. Then, take a break and pamper yourself because you have officially begun writing your proposal.

MEMORIZE YOUR QUESTION/ HYPOTHESIS

In preparation for the defense of your proposal, memorize the official wording of your question/hypothesis. Being able to state it word for word without looking will save you the time and trouble of looking it up repeatedly. It will also help you to automatically filter all the questions and suggestions your committee members make through it. The complete absorption that comes through memorization will ensure you can quickly and effectively steer discussions back on track during the defense.

LITERATURE: MASTERING INFORMATION

While writing and defending your proposal, concentrate on mastering all the implications of the information you have already gathered. If you look up additional sources at this stage, it may introduce conflicting ideas about your methodology, which could then result in writer's block. It may also tempt you to add another thread to your research problem, a thread you will not have time to pursue and still defend on time. Instead, use your reading time to cement the choices you have already made and develop strategies for defending them.

Study your key sources

During the Read stage, you were encouraged to designate appropriate sources as key sources and share them with your adviser. Review these sources one at a time in detail, both the original sources and all associated notes you took regarding them. This review will not be from the standpoint of gleaning information as previous readings have been. Instead, it will be from the standpoint of how a given source supports your proposed research.

Support the necessity of your research

One of the things you will be defending before you are allowed to proceed with your research is that it is necessary. Necessary does not mean earth-shatteringly vital, merely that results from your research will provide useful information. Support for the necessity of your research should be found within the sources that helped you most while developing your research problem. Make a list of your key sources that directly influenced or laid the groundwork for your choice of study subjects and variables. Keep this list handy during your defense.

Support your choice of methodology

Another thing you will be defending is your choice of methodology. There may be multiple data-collection or analysis techniques that would have been appropriate for answering your question or testing your hypothesis. Why did you settle on using the one(s) included in your proposal? If the answer to this question is, "My adviser/data consultant said so," your proposal defense will not succeed, and you will have to do additional work before continuing with your thesis/dissertation. Instead of taking a chance on scuttling your research before it begins, spend time making a list of your key sources that use similar research types, analytic methods, sample sizes, and underlying assumptions or philosophies. If your adviser or data consultant introduced you to any sources during the development of your methodology, make sure you include them. Keep this list handy during your defense as well.

REVIEW SUCCESSFUL PROPOSALS FROM YOUR DEPARTMENT

Pull out two copies of successful proposals you obtained when you wrote your title. Read through them. They will help you embed the diction and structure you will be required to produce yourself. While you read, ask yourself:

- How many sources does each proposal use to support the research's necessity?
- How do the sources walk the reader through the process from topic to research problem?
- How many sources does each proposal use to support the methodology?
- How finely do the proposals break down and support each element of the methodology?
- How many pages are these proposals?
- How do these proposals format the title page?
- How do these proposals format the citation of sources?
- How do these proposals format the presentation of methodology?
- Are there any graphical elements included in the proposals, such as sketches or tables?

By the time you complete this activity, have a mental image of the proposal you are required to produce. If your brain is already generating phrases or sentences for your own proposal, jot them down so you can incorporate them into the final document.

ASSISTANCE: PROVING YOUR SKILLS

Unlike previous stages, assistance will be thin during the Proposal stage. Only you can write the proposal document. Only you can study for, present, and answer questions at your proposal defense. This does not mean the system is designed to throw as many roadblocks in your way to see if you quit. It is more of a way for faculty members to figure out if you have mastered enough research skills to move on in the process or if you need to brush up a little more before you continue. Limited help is available, however, if you know where to look.

Adviser as chair of the committee

If your proposal defense is a formal one that includes the rest of your committee, your adviser will act as chair of the committee. This means that your adviser will control the agenda of the meeting, rephrase any questions you do not understand, and steer off-topic discussions back on target. As chair, your adviser should also monitor the tone of the meeting to ensure it stays professional and courteous. The proposal defense is not designed to be a fight for the ability to begin research but a demonstration that the research is ready to begin. Be sure you understand what you are and are not responsible for regarding the flow of the meeting; then, trust your adviser to hold up his or her end of things.

Committee as source of fine-tuning

You chose the members of your committee based on the benefit your research will derive from their skill sets. As such, they should be considered assets, so you can meet their suggestions and reservations with an open mind. They might see weaknesses in your approach because of their experience, weaknesses that your adviser did not see because he or she is not as experienced within the area in question. Rather than viewing these suggestions and reservations as roadblocks, view them as opportunities to fine-tune your research problem and methodology. When this fine-tuning is done prior to the start of data collection, results are more reliable than when this fine-tuning is done in response to unforeseen problems. You asked these people to serve on your committee for a reason. Remind yourself what those reasons are, and celebrate when the related situations occur.

Graduate student survival tips

Talk to graduate students in your peer network who have successfully defended their proposals, especially those who have members of your committee on their committees. Make these discussions as informal as possible so it does not seem like you are interrogating your peers. Ask if they would share their proposal-defense experiences and offer to take them out for coffee — or beverage of their choice. During these informal discussions:

- Try to keep things light and anecdotal.
- Promise them nothing they say will be repeated by you to anyone. Make sure you keep this promise because you will need their advice again when it comes time to defend your completed thesis/ dissertation.
- To ensure confidentiality, do not take notes.
- If a discussion takes an extremely negative turn, find a gracious way to either change the focus to a positive angle on the topic or change the subject altogether.

Your goal for these informal events is to dispel the mystery surrounding the process. Not knowing what you face is a source for anxiety, but anxiety is the last thing you need right now. If you are having trouble getting the discussion started with your peers, consider kicking things off with the following questions:

- How long ago did you defend your proposal?
- Did you successfully defend the first time or did you have to change things and try again?
- Who spoke first, and how did you know when you were supposed to start?
- Did anything go brilliantly that you had been worried about?

- Were there any disasters? How did you overcome them?
- Were you able to answer all their questions? What did you say when you did not know the answers? What did they say?
- What did you wear?
- How long did the whole meeting take?

Again, this is not an interrogation. No matter how anxious you are to get the answer to these questions and more, do not fire them at your peers like a batting-practice machine fires baseballs. Ask one question, and see where the conversation leads. Your peers should have funny stories to share. These stories may include some tense moments, but that is what makes them exciting because you already know they have the happy ending of a successful defense.

Extra help for ESL students

If English is your second language, then the written form of the proposal may pose extra challenges for you. Understanding academic English is one thing, producing it is another. It is beyond the scope of your adviser's duties to tutor you in the fine points of grammar and sentence structure, so consider getting tutoring from the on-campus writing center. The international student center on your campus may also have a list of writing-assistance resources. Accessing this help will mean you will spend more time on the written portion of your proposal than other students. Composition and revision will take longer and will involve more people. Do not be surprised if a writing tutor says that a passage is great, but your adviser has problems with it. The tutor is speaking from a written-conventions standpoint, while your adviser is speaking from a content standpoint. Just as writing instruction is beyond the scope of your adviser's duties, content instruction is beyond the scope of your writing tutor's duties.

DATA: COLLECTION CONSIDERATIONS

By this point in your discussions with your adviser and data consultant, you should be settled on a methodology. You know what kind of data you plan to collect, as well as how you will collect and analyze it. You have also developed data-collection instruments. If possible, take a moment with some practice data — information that will not be used in your research — and try using the instrument so you can answer questions about its use with first-hand experience. Sources of practice data could be journal articles, public data from government agency websites, documentary videos, or any other multimedia source that mimics the kind of data you would like to collect.

As you finalize and write the methodology section of your proposal, you will need to finalize the logistics of your research. Although you may not be able to get binding commitments yet, you should at least have verbal agreements that these logistics should be approved soon. Your committee will want some kind of reassurance that if they approve your methodology, you will be able to access the things you need to complete the research.

Sources of assistants and subjects

Chapter 4 walked you through suggestions on where to find study subjects. If you still have not found a source of the types of people/organisms/things you need for your study, work with your adviser on a plan to fix this. He or she may need to call in a few favors to get you connected with someone willing to help.

Depending on the scope and intensity of your proposed data-collection process, you may want to ask people to volunteer as assistants. Undergraduates in their junior or senior year may be willing to take independent study for a semester and help you under the supervision of your adviser. You may also be able to get some fellow graduate students to assist with your data collection, especially if you have already helped them collect theirs. If you only need help for a day or two, you could also post help-wanted fliers on the departmental bulletin board (physical or electronic). However, safety and quality-control concerns will be harder to address when using strangers. A better plan would be to contact on-campus clubs or honor societies that pertain to your discipline and to ask them to put you in touch with respected members who might be willing to help.

Cost and sources of funding

Regardless of whether you think the cost of your research is high, prepare a budget for it. Practicing the estimation of costs and searching for funding to meet those costs will help you in the future when you need to apply for grants or to ask your company to allocate funds. Budgets normally list income and expenses by category. In this case, income would be funding from any source applied to cover research expenses. This will be money from your personal funds, gifts from a rich uncle who believes in what you are doing, any grant money you may have acquired, or any funds the university earmarks for graduate student research. Expenses would be the costs of everything associated with your research from photocopies to overnight stays. The following is a sample list of expense categories that may be adjusted to fit your situation:

- Administrative costs (application fees, membership fees, postage, data backup expenses)
- Literature costs (photocopies, purchase of books/articles, journal subscriptions)
- Equipment costs (rental or purchase of data-collection instruments, software, hardware, and other physical items needed for your research)
- Travel costs (mileage to and from your research location, lodging, meals, passport fees, car rental)
- Assistance costs (extrinsic rewards for study participants and assistants, consultant fees, thank you gifts for your adviser and committee members)

How detailed you list things out within each category is up to you, but it should be detailed enough for you to know which receipts go with which categories later on. Total all these expenses, and compare that total with the estimated income. Is there more income than expense? If so, then you may relax as long as you plan to keep tracking expenses closely. Is there more expense than income? If so, budget shortfalls will come out of your pocket. Either way, find ways to trim expenses or continue to look for additional research funding.

WORKING WITH OVERSIGHT AGENCIES AND INDIVIDUALS

Depending on the kind of study subjects from which you will collect data, you may need to coordinate with additional people beyond your adviser and committee. It is vital for you to find and contact these additional people as soon as possible, even if it is not yet time to start any official proceedings. It will take you some time to get oriented to and meet these requirements, so starting now will ensure you are ready to go when your committee approves your methodology.

Human research

The complexity of human research was already discussed in Chapter 4. Take a moment to review where you are in the IRB application process. Follow up with the departmental coordinator to see if it is time for you to apply or if there is anything missing from an application you have already submitted. If you have already applied and the application was rejected, work with the IRB coordinator and your adviser to resolve these issues before your research time period gets extended beyond your personal tolerances.

Animal research

If your study involves animal subjects, as some research questions involving biology or psychology will, there may be someone who oversees the treatment of these animals. This oversight is most formal with vertebrate subjects (animals with an internal skeleton of bone or cartilage). Work with your adviser to navigate these oversight processes. If your study subjects are housed at a zoo or animal research laboratory, you will have to work under the supervision of the animals' handler. Work in a conscientious manner, and follow all guidelines. If you cut corners, these people are less likely to agree to let the next graduate student work with their animals. You will also damage your ability to use these handlers as references when you are looking for new research/employment opportunities.

Property owners

If your study involves field work, as some research questions involving biology or geology will, someone will own the property that houses your study subjects. This may be a governmental agency, a nonprofit organization, a business, or an individual. Understand that none of these types of owners has to grant you access to their property. Be respectful and professional when making your request. If they seem hesitant, gently ask what their concerns are, and show your willingness to address them. Let them know you would be happy to abide by a list of ground rules and/or sign a liability waiver. There may be some concerns you will not be able to overcome; for instance, a farmer's worry you will find an endangered species on the land which will limit his use of his own land. Accepting ahead of time that your research may not be a good fit for the land owner will help you graciously thank the owner for his or her time and move on to the next possibility. You will have far fewer conflicts with property owners while conducting your research if they truly are happy to have you there.

WRITTEN WORK: THE PROPOSAL

Depending on the degree you seek and your department, the written proposal may be a multi-chaptered document or a short document with a few sections. You should know by this point what kind of document you are expected to write because you reviewed successful proposals from your department. Find out how your multi-page document should be bound.

It may be as simple as a staple in the upper left-hand corner or as complex as comb binding. Even though the proposal is not your finished thesis/dissertation, it is an official and important document that will be read by busy faculty members. It should be clean and professional looking to show your respect for the process and the committee's time.

Typical proposal complexity

As stated above, the length and organization of the proposal is affected by the final research document produced. The complexity of the information presented is also affected by this. By necessity, the more complex the document is expected to be, the longer it will be because there needs to be enough space to properly introduce and support thoughts. Theses are normally shorter than dissertations, but total length of either document varies by department and research approach.

Thesis

The thesis proposal has the potential to become the first portion of your thesis with a bit of verb-tense revision. Take the writing of it seriously, even if you only have to present it to your adviser in an informal meeting. Your written and verbal proposal should demonstrate a level of proficiency with academic thought and an understanding of your proposed methodology. Note that the level here is proficiency — a sign that you are ready for your academic apprenticeship.

Dissertation

Typically, the dissertation proposal will become the first three chapters of the dissertation — with some verb-tense changes and other minor revisions. With this in mind, make sure the thoughts you present in your proposal demonstrate mastery of the background material for your topic. The level of questions asked at your proposal defense is likely to be highly complex as well, especially in terms of your methodology. As a doctoral candidate, you are expected to have a deeper understanding of your topic and how to design research than someone pursuing a master's degree.

Proposal style guidelines

The written proposal is a document governed by your department's preferred style guide, a guide you identified in the Design stage. But, this published style guide may not include items peculiar to proposals at your university. Fortunately, you have already built a model thesis/dissertation while working through Chapter 2 and taken notes on the shape of successful proposals while working through this chapter. Both of these activities have helped you develop an informal style guide you can use to fill in the gaps from the published manuals. Although you do not want to copy wording from these models, you do want to refer to them when you are stuck and have questions.

Function

The function of the written proposal is two-fold. The first part is to act as a training ground for writing in the academic style. This training includes diction, clarity, use of sources to support the opening of an argument, and proper citation technique. The second part is to communicate the who, what, where, when, why, and how of the research you would like to engage in as part of your degree requirements. Learning to communicate these concepts effectively and persuade a committee to approve them will enable you to propose research to future academic partners, employers, and grant committees.

Verb tense and tone

When writing a thesis or dissertation, you will use either active or passive voice. Your adviser should be able to assist you in deciding which tense to use, as it will depend on your subject matter. If you are writing a journalism thesis, you are more likely to use active voice than if writing a scientific thesis.

In passive voice, the subjects of sentences are acted upon rather than completing an action. For instance, "Evidence of parasite infestation was not recorded" is passive, while, "We did not record evidence of parasite infestation" would be active. Passive voice lends a more objective tone to academic documents and lessens the chance of wording things in a way that will imply causation where none has been proven. It also tends toward long and complex phrases, which is one reason people find the academic style difficult and/or dry to read. But, after reading all your sources, you should be more comfortable reading this style. You probably also have the tone and voice embedded in your head, ready to be reproduced in your own writing.

Some parts of the proposal, such as the statement of the research problem and the methodology, will be written in future tense because the research has not happened yet. Other parts, such as the literature review and other sentences referring to your sources, will be written in past tense because that research has already happened. If this seems confusing to you, look over one of the proposals you read in the previous section and specifically look for sentences with past versus future tense.

Formatting

Formatting varies, so make sure to check your model proposals for an appropriate look and feel. Look for the use of font size, bold, italics, capitalization, and indentation in the following proposal elements:

- Title page
- Author information
- Chapter headings

- Section headings
- Quotations
- Citations
- Footnotes and endnotes
- Graphics and captions

However you choose to format your proposal, the important thing is to be consistent throughout the document. This will allow your committee members to find the relationships and hierarchies of the information you are presenting if you have inadvertently used formatting your committee would consider nonstandard.

Proposal contents

Whether you are writing a multi-chaptered document or a ten-page report-style document, all proposals should contain the same three elements: a statement of the problem, a review of pertinent literature, and a proposed methodology. The contents of your proposal must communicate *what* you want to research, *why* you want to research it, and *how* you plan to research it. The written proposal also prepares your committee members for their participation in your research and serves as a starting point for discussion.

Statement of problem with background

You have already written the statement of your research problem in the form of a question or hypothesis. This statement can either open this section or close it, depending on your personal writing style. If you open this section with your statement, then your rationale will be presented afterward with support from your key sources. All your thoughts will flow from your research statement. If you close this section with your statement, your thoughts and rationale will flow toward your research statement with support from your key sources. Either way, everything you write in this section should answer the question, "What do I want to research?"

Literature review

You have read and utilized far more sources to design your research than just your key sources. There are numerous supporting sources in your notes that have lent their findings to the minutiae of your design. You have had to weigh multiple views on points of fact and methodologies. You have decided which ones you feel are stronger and found even more sources to justify those decisions. The literature review is more than an annotated bibliography. It is a synthesis of all the sources that have led you to this particular research design. Introduce and describe essential points of background and methodology through the conclusions of the literature. Sources that agree on points should be presented together and then contrasted with sources that disagree on the same points. The order in which you present these points should flow in a logical progression that will lead readers from the background of your research problem to your proposed methodology. While you write this section, focus on the question, "Why do I want to research this?"

Proposed methodology

You have already designed your methodology. Now is the time to communicate that design in writing. This section is intended to describe every aspect of data collection and analysis so your methodology can be optimized before you begin. When it is incorporated into your thesis/dissertation, it will also serve the purpose of relaying enough information so another researcher could repeat your study to confirm your results. As such, organize tasks and considerations in chronological order. You will also include copies of any surveys, forms, or other data-collection instruments and refer to them from within the text. Make sure to include a detailed description of your study subjects and research location. Give the steps that will be involved in collecting data, including any rewards that participants may be given. Walk through the planned analysis method and the rationale for that choice. If you experience any anxiety or writer's block while writing this section, take a breath and remind yourself that everything in this section answers the question, "How do I plan to research this?"

Bibliography

Even though your proposal contains a review of the literature, you still need to include a bibliography. Hopefully, you stored your bibliography data in an Excel spreadsheet or the OpenOffice Bibliography Database mentioned in Chapter 1. If not, you will need to build your bibliography from scratch. Your bibliography should be placed behind your proposal sections/chapters. Each source you referenced and used should be listed. Include complete bibliographic information for each source, which should be formatted according to your department's preferred style guide. Frequently, a bibliography will be sorted alphabetically by the first author's last name with the first line of text touching the left margin and the rest of the auto-wrapped lines tabbed in half an inch. Typing in all your sources' bibliographic information from scratch is time-consuming, so allow yourself several hours to find, type, and format this essential piece of your proposal (and the future thesis/dissertation).

If you stored your bibliography in an Excel spreadsheet, you will need to perform a mail merge operation in order to generate your bibliography. To do this:

1. Look in your spreadsheet to make sure your headers are named meaningfully such as "Author Name 1" or "Section/Article Title." If not, rename them so you will know which fields to include later in the merge. Also, be sure your sources are listed alphabetically by first author before moving on to Step 2.

2. In an empty Word document, select Tools > Letters and Mailings > Mail Merge. This will bring up a mail merge tool bar, typically in a right-hand column.

3. Under "Select document type," choose Directory, and then click "Next."

4. Under "Select starting document," choose "Use the current document," and then click "Next."

5. Under "Select recipients," choose "Use an existing list," then browse to the spreadsheet file that contains your bibliographic data. Click once on that file, and then click "Open."

6. In the "Select a table" dialog box, click on the choice that contains the data you need. This might be a tab within a multi-tabbed spreadsheet or the spreadsheet as a whole. Click "OK."

7. In the "Mail Merge Recipients" box, uncheck any of the entries you do not want included in your bibliography, and then click "OK." Then click "Next."

8. Under "Arrange your directory," choose "More items." This will bring up a box that lists all your headers.

9. Insert your headers (in the same order that the information should print according to your style guide) by clicking on a header and then clicking "Insert." When you are finished inserting fields, click "Close."

10. You will have a string of fields that look something like: <<Author_Name1>><<Author_Name2>> <<Author_Name3>><<year>><<ArticleChapter_Title>> <<JournalBook_Title>><<VolumeEdition>><<PagesPlace>>

11. Format the string of fields so it has all the spaces and punctuation it will need to match the style guide. At the end of the string, be sure to hit the "Enter" or "Return" key so your cursor is on the next line. This should look something like: <<Author_Name1>>, <<Author_Name2>> and <<Author_Name3>>. <<year>>. "<<ArticleChapter_Title>>," <<JournalBook_Title>>, <<VolumeEdition>>, <<PagesPlace>>. You may need to tweak the punctuation

in the finished product if some of your sources are of an unusual kind.

12. Be sure the margins and indents are set the way they will need to be for your bibliography.

13. When all your fields are in place and your formatting is set, click "Next." Then click "Next: Complete the merge."

14. Under "Merge," select "To New Document," and then click "Next."

15. Under "Merge to New Document," select All and click "OK."

16. A new document should pop up that has all your sources listed in alphabetical order with nearly perfect formatting.

To fix glaring format errors, return to the original merge document and keep clicking "Previous" until you get to the stage where you can correct the formatting of the fields. Then, retrace your steps, and merge again. To fix minor errors in a few special sources, just correct them in the finished document. Be sure to save this merged document and the field-layout document so you can easily alter them later when creating the final bibliography for your thesis/dissertation.

If you used the OpenOffice Bibliography Database to store your bibliographic data, review the tutorial by Don Peterson from the Tutorials for OpenOffice website (**www.tutorialsforopenoffice.org/tutorial/Bibliographies.html**) that was presented in Chapter 1. Properly formatting your bibliography using this tool is a detailed process beyond the scope of this book; however, following this tutorial step by step will get you where you need to go. Although you do have to invest more time in learning how to use this application, the benefit comes as you further your research post-graduation and write additional papers that use these same sources.

DEFENDING THE PROPOSAL

Whether you are presenting to your adviser alone or to your entire committee, the proposal defense is your chance to continue the academic argument introduced in the written proposal. This oral forum allows you to discuss your academic argument by presenting your intentions, explaining unclear passages, straightening out misunderstandings, and demonstrating your readiness to embark on the next phase of your research. The public speaking aspect of this step is intimidating, even to people who routinely speak in front of people for their jobs. There is a lot riding on the presentation. But, at the end of the day, everyone in your audience will be there playing their part to move your research forward. They want to approve your proposal; they just might have some helpful comments along the way.

Presentation

Before the committee can ask you clarifying questions, you must first make the oral presentation of your proposal. Plan your presentation with the same look and feel to the departmental seminars you have attended. Although you will not have data to present, you will be presenting the research problem, its rationale, and methodology in a similar way. Ask your adviser how long this initial presentation should take so you may plan to relay the proper amount of detail. You should have at least 20 minutes to get through your initial presentation uninterrupted; it would be a good idea to find good stopping places along the way to ask the committee if they have any questions before you move on. This way you will be able to control the timing of interruptions in your presentation flow and not get lost in your notes while answering questions.

Revisions

Make no mistake: You will have revisions to do after your proposal defense. Be sure to bring a notepad and pen with you to record the revisions agreed upon by the committee. Your adviser may also meet with you after the official meeting to discuss these revisions in more detail. Feel free to take some time to decompress after the meeting, but try to revise your proposal file to reflect the changes as soon as you can. You do not want to forget the nuances of the changes before you have them worded appropriately. If the committee asks you to do extra reading before making a revision, be sure to show the extra sources and the completed revisions to your adviser. Find out whether the rest of the committee wants a copy of the revised proposal as well.

Scheduling your proposal defense

The proposal defense is a lengthy meeting that takes hours of preparation for your committee members, not to mention for yourself. Do your committee members the courtesy of scheduling your proposal with enough advance notice that everyone involved can do a thorough job preparing and reshuffle their regular duties with limited inconvenience. When attempting to schedule the defense, ask your adviser for a list of available dates that he or she thinks are a reasonable target. Once you have this list, check it against your own schedule. If you have an unchangeable conflict on a particular date, cross it off. If you have conflicts that could be rescheduled, leave them on the list for now. E-mail the rest of your committee, and ask them which of the potential dates work best for them. This step may take a bit of negotiation, but do the best you can. If a particular committee member has a packed calendar you cannot seem to schedule around, ask your adviser to contact that member and find an alternate that will work. If no alternate can be found, see if the member can attend via speaker phone or video conferencing utility.

Preparing for your proposal defense

You have met with peers to get oriented in the way this event will occur. You have prepared the formal written document. You have scheduled the defense. If your proposal defense includes your entire committee, then your adviser has also determined the document is at least ready for presentation to others. Most of the remaining organization needed prior to the big day is for you to do alone. But, there are two organizational tasks that involve others.

Meeting with your adviser

Schedule a short meeting with your adviser to make sure the two of you are in sync regarding the research you will propose and how you will propose it. This meeting may take place in any form convenient to your adviser: in person, on the phone, via a chat client, or even by online video conference through Skype™ (**www.skype.com**). You have already agreed on the final document, so your oral presentation should mirror that format. It never hurts to get a feel for how your adviser expects you to organize the information and which points he or she is most keen for you to highlight. It is also a good time to discover what concerns your adviser still has so you may prepare ways to address those concerns during the defense.

Submitting your proposal to your committee in advance

Ask your adviser how far in advance to give the final draft of your proposal to your committee members. To show you value them and are considerate of their time, this should be at least a week before the meeting. Print clean copies with a good-quality printer on paper at least 25-pound weight. Cotton-content paper might be a bit overboard, but it does allow for lots of handling without looking crumpled and dingy.

It is also a good idea to make a portable document format (PDF) version of your proposal. That way, if committee members lose the printed version, you can quickly e-mail another copy they can print. If you are using OpenOffice for your word processing, you may make a PDF by clicking on the red and white square that says "PDF." If you are using Microsoft Word on a computer that also has Adobe Acrobat installed, you will be able to click on a similar PDF icon to generate one. If you are using Microsoft

Word and you do not have PDF generating capabilities, you may install a free PDF generator called PrimoPDF®:

1. In your favorite Web browser, type in the URL **www. primopdf.com**.

2. Click on the "Free Download" button. Be aware that on the same page will be a button for "Free 14 Day Trial," but that is for a fee-based product called NitroPDF Professional. Make sure you click on the button that will download PrimoPDF instead.

3. Clicking on the download button will take you to the CNET's approved download site. Click the "Download Now" button, and follow the on-screen instructions, which will vary depending on the operating system you use.

Once you have PrimoPDF installed, you may make PDFs from Word documents by:

1. Choosing File > Print

2. From the dropdown box at the top of the printer settings, select "PrimoPDF."

3. Click the "OK" button.

4. PrimoPDF will open up a dialog box. Across the top are some colored choices. Choose "Screen."

5. There are two dropdown boxes. The first is labeled "Save As." Choose "Ask when creating PDF." This will allow you to choose the file name and folder your PDF will be saved in.

6. The second dropdown box is labeled "Post Process." Choose "Open PDF." This will open the finished PDF file after it is created so you may check for errors.

When you have completed these steps, the PDF version of your proposal is ready for distribution. You may now attach it to an e-mail and send it to any committee members who would like it. If any of your committee members use an e-book reader, ask if they would like a PDF copy in addition to the printed copy. They will be able to easily view a PDF on their e-book devices. Even if they have a first-generation Kindle™ and need to perform a small conversion process, they will appreciate the convenience and the thought.

ORGANIZATION: SUPPORTING THE PROPOSAL

Out of all the reading you have done, all the notes you have taken, and all the correspondence you have written up to now, how do you decide which information to bring to your proposal defense? You cannot possibly bring it all. And even if you could, you would not want to because struggling into the defense room with stacks of information would make for a less-than-graceful entrance. Instead, the first impression you want to make is of a professional, organized, and focused researcher-in-training who is confident in his or her ability to prepare a presentation. The less nervous you appear, the more relaxed the committee will be. But, nerves are natural with new experiences, so this section will help you organize your materials in a way that will prevent fumbling with and digging for supporting documents and visual aids.

Printed copy of proposal

Regardless of the binding type you used on the printed proposals you distributed, turn your single-sided copy into a three-hole punched document, and place it in a separate one-inch binder. This will allow you to quickly flip from one page to the next when the committee asks you questions. It will also prevent you from accidentally getting the pages out of order like a loose stack in a file folder would. A stapled version will require you to pick it up in order to manipulate it. A comb bound version would lie flat like one in a binder, but it would not allow you to instantly insert additional note sheets generated during the meeting into the pages for which they pertain. Consider marking the major sections of your proposal with removable sticky arrows/notes and bring extras to the meeting so you can flag sections your committee asks you to revise as they ask you to revise them.

Notes

Put together an outline of what you plan to say when you present your proposed research. You may organize your remarks like you organized your written proposal. However, the bulk of your time should be spent on laying the groundwork for your research problem and presenting your proposed methodology. You may present some of the sources from your literature review, but they should be mentioned in conjunction with the other two elements — research problem and methodology — rather than presented on their own.

Store this outline in the same binder that holds your copy of the proposal. It should either be tucked in a pocket built into the binder cover or stored in a three-hole punched folder on top of your proposal copy. This way you can pull out your presentation outline, set it on the table or lectern, and still be able to flip through the pages of your proposal as needed without losing your place in the outline.

If you know of areas in your written proposal in which you will have to justify your decisions, for instance if you have chosen a nonstandard research method, make notes that summarize everything that went into the decision. These decision notes should be written in an orderly fashion that shows a logical progression from conception to decision, including elements from meetings with your adviser, meetings with your consultants, and key sources you have read. Restrict the length of decision notes to one page using phrases and keywords rather than complete sentences. Three-hole punch the right side of these decision notes, and place them in your binder to the left of the pages to which they pertain.

Visual aids

At some point in your career during this electronic age, you will be expected to make a presentation rich in visual media. At the very least, you will be expected to include visuals in your final thesis/dissertation defense. Find out what kind of presentation technology you have access to, and learn how to use it now for your proposal so you are comfortable with it when it comes time for your final defense. Passing a photo/graph hard copy around the room will cause distractions, not to mention the visual aid will be seen out of sync with its associated oral information. The rest of this section will describe the devices you may have available and introduce you to their use.

Overhead projectors use a light bulb under a glass plate to shine light through a transparency (clear plastic sheet) to a head with a mirror that then bounces the image onto a projector screen. These projectors may be considered "old school," but they are easier to use than computerized devices. To make transparencies, you will need a box of transparency sheets and a printer. Make sure the sheets you buy are the correct type for the printer you will use. Once you have your sheets:

1. Open up a new word-processing document. This document should be constructed in "portrait" mode instead of "landscape," so it is taller than it is wide.

2. Type up any main points you want to project. Be sure to use a large font — 18 point and higher — and include no more than three ideas per page. Refrain from using fancy fonts, as they can be hard to read if the projector does not focus pin-sharp.

3. Insert any pictures or graphs you would like to share, one image per page. Pictures to share might be of your study site, a special apparatus, or any other photograph/sketch that will help your committee understand who/what you will be researching. Graphs to share might be flow charts, diagrams, or any other visual representation of information that will

help your committee understand how the research will be done and why you want to do it.

4. Once the word-processing document contains all your visuals, load the transparency sheets into your printer. These sheets have a smooth side and a rough side. All printers are different, so be sure to follow the directions that come with your sheets for determining which side to face up in the paper tray.

5. In your word-processing software, click File > Print. Look for a "media type" or "paper type" dropdown box and choose "transparencies." Click "OK."

6. Print the transparencies. You will have the best luck if you print each page one at a time. This will cut down on sheets getting jammed or taking up multiple sheets at the same time.

7. Print a paper copy of your visuals as well. Lay each transparency on its matching paper; three-hole punch them, and place them in presentation order in your binder with your presentation notes.

Document cameras work with a computer and digital projector to display physical objects on a projector screen. The same kind of text and images as those listed for overheads can be assembled in a word-processing document, but you do not have to print these pages on transparency sheets. Instead, they may be printed directly onto paper. In addition, document cameras can project three-dimensional objects on the screen. They magnify and project anything that fits on the working surface and does not exceed the focal length for the camera, which is embedded in a suspended head much like an overhead projector. The directions for use will depend on the document camera, computer, and projector, so be sure to get instructions from the department's audio-visual (AV) expert. If you plan to use a document camera, three-hole punch and file any papers you are going to project in your binder in presentation order. If you will be using three-dimensional objects as well, store them in a nice box, and jot a note to yourself such as "display _____ here," and file it in the binder with your other presentation notes.

Digital slideshows are created in computer software, played on a computer, and displayed through a digital projector. Although preparing your visuals this way gives you the potential of producing a slick and media-rich presentation, it can also lure you into producing a visual nightmare. Multiple flying text effects, blinking icons, and gratuitous sound effects have absolutely no place in an academic presentation of this nature. If you have the desire and/or skills to produce a Microsoft PowerPoint or OpenOffice Impress slideshow, remember to present one visual message at a time. Think minimalism. An excellent resource for the design of your slides is *Slide:ology: the Art and Science of Creating Great Presentations* by Nancy Duarte. Although digital slideshows will let people see how technically savvy you are, they are vulnerable to technical glitches. Some of the potential scenarios include:

- **Problem:** You saved your slideshow to a flash drive, but you left your flash drive at home or the flash drive is not working properly.

  - **How to avoid:** E-mail a copy of your slideshow to a Web-based e-mail account the night before your defense so you can download it at school on a loaner flash drive.

- **Problem:** Your equipment request got preempted by a faculty member's need, so the computer/projector combination you need to display your file is not available after all.

  - **How to avoid:** Print your slides as handouts (four slides per page) the night before so you can dash out to a copy place to make a printed packet for each committee member.

- **Problem:** You are halfway through with your presentation when the projector bulb blows.

- **How to avoid:** Print any image or graph slides one per page the night before so you can hold them up while you refer to them and then pass them around the room.

- **Problem:** You are halfway through your presentation when the computer decides to do an operating-system update and restarts.

  - **How to avoid:** Before you begin your presentation, ask a technically savvy faculty member or the AV expert to turn automatic updates off or to postpone them for a few hours.

Technology is supposed to make life simpler. Make a plan to share visuals with the device you are comfortable using. The last thing you want is to spend so much time wrestling with your visuals that you do not have time to practice delivering your presentation. Also, find out if there is a departmental AV staff person who you must make arrangements with to deliver or unlock equipment. Some departments have AV team members who will run the equipment during the meeting. There may be fees or deposits required for these services, but they will be well worth it. Be sure to pack your visual aids, and set the container by your door the night before the meeting so you do not forget them.

Note-taking materials

After your presentation is finished, there will be discussion. By the time the discussion ends, you should have a proposal that has been either approved or approved pending revision. If it is approved pending revision, you will definitely need to take notes so you can accurately revise. If it is approved as written, you will still want to take some notes because your committee members will have brought up some good points that will need to be considered while writing the finished thesis/dissertation. The note-taking materials you choose will depend on the preferences you identified in the Organization section of Chapter 1. Some combinations to consider are:

- **One pack of sticky-flags, one pack of sticky notes, and a pencil/ pen.** Use the sticky-flags to point to notes you write in the margins of your proposal. You can also write your notes on sticky notes, let them hang beyond the edge of the paper, and mark the location of the information.

- **Notepad and pencil/pen.** Take all your notes on the notepad, recording the proposal page number that each note corresponds to. Three-hole punch these notes after the meeting, and file them in the binder.

- **Laptop computer.** This option only works if you already own one and you will be allowed to sit down during the discussion period. Open up your proposal file in your word processor. Place your cursor near the section in question, and then select "Insert > Comment" (in either Microsoft Word or OpenOffice Writer). Type in the committee's suggestion or question.

No matter what kind of note-taking materials you choose to use, test them prior to the meeting. Test that your pens have ink. Sharpen your wooden pencils, or bring extra leads for your mechanical pencils. Practice inserting comments in your word-processing file. Make sure you have enough sticky-flags or sticky-notes to get you through an enthusiastic discussion. You might also consider a color-coding system for them. Above all, make sure your note-taking materials are packed in your bag the night before so they are not forgotten in a bout of last-minute nerves.

Final preparations for your defense

Now that you have your materials prepared for presenting your proposal, it is time to get yourself prepared. All the notes and visuals in the world will add up to nothing if you rush into the meeting with a chaotic mind. You will need enough focus to access all the presentation aids you have prepared and be able to track questions accurately. Do not skimp on this section. Give it as much attention as you gave the previous one.

Practicing your presentation

Different people have different presentation styles. Some like to memorize their presentations with precision, to the point of memorizing complete sentences. Others like to memorize the bones of their presentations but flesh them out with contemporaneous speaking. By now, you should know what your preferences are. Do not try to practice a style that goes against your natural preference; instead, play to your strengths. If you are the memorizing type, write up your presentation based on the notes you sketched in the previous section, and commit them to memory. If you are the contemporaneous type, practice connecting the phrases in your presentation notes orally several times to find your flow.

Either way, be sure to practice the final version of your presentation out loud at least twice. Use a timer or clock to see how long your presentation takes. Is it within the acceptable time range? If not, find areas to trim/expand so it fits. Be aware that you will most likely talk faster once you are in front of your audience because of adrenaline. If your practiced version comes in just at the lower end of your target time range, consider adding a bit more to account for this.

Getting yourself in the right frame of mind

Of course it would be marvelous if you could know the questions your committee members will ask you ahead of time, but that would defeat the purpose of evaluating your research readiness. Instead of stressing out about studying every source you have read so you can give all perfect answers, briefly review your key sources, and focus on your proposed research. Of all the people in the meeting room, you will be the one who will have spent the most time thinking about your research problem and working through a possible methodology. Although the faculty members on your committee are more experienced in the process of research than you are, you are more experienced than they are with your particular problem. Tell yourself this every time you start to worry, especially when facing your committee on that day. Focus on the portion of your defense you can control, and let the questions take care of themselves.

Relaxing and getting some sleep

Whatever you do, do not pull an all-nighter in order to prepare for your proposal defense. You need to be well rested in order to pack without forgetting anything, think without getting confused, and respond without reacting. Try not to cram during the morning before your defense if you can help it, either. Instead, take a bubble bath or a brisk walk or anything else that helps you relax. You have worked extremely hard already, so trust that all your previous effort has prepared you for the task at hand.

FINAL TIPS ON DEFENDING YOUR PROPOSAL

When you are actually defending your proposal, try not to rush your initial presentation. Take your time, and be sure to breathe. Have some water with you in case your throat gets dry or you begin to cough. If you are worried about what to do with your hands, keeping a pen (with a cap) on the lectern with your notes will give you a nondistracting object to fidget with if needed. It will also give you a way to mark your place in your notes if someone asks you a question during the initial presentation. Try to have fun with your presentation if you can. After all, you get to talk at length to a captive audience about a subject you love.

During the discussion period, listen carefully to the question asked. Keep your answers as short and specific as you can, and wait for any follow-up questions. If you do not know the answer to a question, do not try to make one up. Simply say, "That is an interesting question, and I will have to look into it." Stay as calm as you can, even if a question feels threatening to your research and/or your degree. You are under a lot of pressure and your perceptions may not be accurate. Focus on responding to the academic question and not to any perceived intent of the question. The main purpose for this gathering is for you to explain what you would like to study, why you would like to study it, and how you would like to go about it. Focus on that purpose, and everyone else will, too.

CASE STUDY: MAKE A CONTRIBUTION

Prof. I. Hal Sudborough
Department of Computer Science
Erik Jonsson School of Engineering
and Computer Science
University of Texas at Dallas
hal_sud@yahoo.com

BIOGRAPHY:

After earning his doctorate in Computer Science from Penn State University in 1971, Dr. Sudborough joined the faculty of the Electronic Engineering/Computer Science Department of Northwestern University in Chicago, Illinois, where he received tenure and was promoted through the ranks to the position of full professor. In 1985, he became a Founders Professor in the Computer Science Department at the University of Texas at Dallas, where he continues to serve.

DISSERTATION TITLE AND SYNOPSIS:

Computation by Multi-Head Writing Automata

This dissertation contained a characterization of the computing power of finite state machines with multiple one-way read/write heads on a single tape.

FIRST-PERSON ACCOUNT:

As an adviser/committee member for scores of students, the most common weakness of students' research proposals is the lack of clarity in writing and the lack of adequate detail in definitions and proofs. In addition, there is often a lack of confidence in their self-perceived ability to solve open problems in the field. The most effective way to address the latter problem is to work closely with students and show them how progress can be made. To address the language difficulties, I usually ask the students to make presentations to the research group and give suggestions/corrections.

The typical writing problems of their dissertations are addressed by my reading the dissertations several times and making iterative suggestions and corrections. It is an exhausting procedure.

If I could give one tip to graduate students for writing a successful thesis/ dissertation, it would be: Make a fundamental contribution to the field — a contribution noticed by researchers/colleagues all over the world. For my advisees, this requires me to provide a good deal of coaching and counseling, as most students I've mentored have little confidence in their ability to solve significant open problems. It seems to be an issue of low self-esteem, perhaps as a result of a long and often painful process of competitive classes and mass education with too little time and opportunity to exhibit often dormant creative and intellectual ability.

I was in this state myself for the first few years during my doctoral work and continued on even afterward when I was a new assistant professor. I recall with great pleasure, however, making a breakthrough and being able to solve a problem of some interest to the broad community of researchers of which I wanted to be part. The boost to my confidence was electric. I had arrived! From that time on, I never doubted my capability to do scholarly work and make fundamental contributions.

I believe the capability is in all of us; it simply needs encouragement and, of course, hard work to manifest itself. I sometimes feel the need to "prime the pump" with graduate students who I mentor. That is, when they suggest a better solution to an open problem is too difficult or impossible, I work hard myself and find a way to make progress the student and I can share. As a particular example, I had a graduate student a few years ago to whom I suggested improving a result in a published paper. She spent some time looking at it and expressed her opinion that the published result was likely the best one possible. When I disagreed, she bet me $5 on the issue. I then wrote out an algorithm for the conjectured worst case of the problem, which gave a much-improved result. I suggested that she continue on the work by showing that the conjectured worst case was, in fact, the worst case. The result was a nice publication with a much-improved result and a $5 spider plant — which she gave me as payoff — that is still flourishing on the windowsill of my office.

SUMMARY OF TASKS

Phase 1

- Write your proposal, including a title.
- Prepare visual aids for the presentation.
- Memorize your question/hypothesis.
- Talk to others about proposal defense expectations.
- Find a writing tutor if needed.
- Find research assistants if needed.
- Create a budget for your research.
- Schedule your proposal defense.

Phase 2

- Review key and supporting sources.
- Review successful proposals.
- Continue the search for study subjects and research locations.
- Write presentation notes.
- Practice the presentation, including the use of visual aids.
- Attend your proposal defense.

Chapter 6: Test

This chapter will help you stay focused and productive as you test your question/hypothesis. Although you should be an active participant in the testing stage, you may not have to collect every data point yourself or come up with solutions to mishaps in isolation. Training your assistants, developing useful visual aids, designing backup systems, and a keeping detailed log book are tasks that will serve you well during the testing stage, as well as the analysis and writing stages.

TOPIC: REVIEW PERIODICALLY

Once the committee approves your proposal, data collection may begin. If you are ready to test your question/hypothesis by collecting data, you have no critical tasks to complete in regards to topic. But, it is a good idea to periodically review your question/hypothesis during the testing stage to keep the focus on your approved research problem. For example, if you are investigating the use of bees as a 14th century literary device but notice a prevalence of oak references in the same bee-laden documents, you might be tempted to spend time trying to figure out if the two are linked for some reason. Although this would make an excellent follow-up study, it is off topic, and pursuing it will waste time, energy, and resources. By constantly reminding yourself of your approved research problem, you will more easily jot these new avenues down for inclusion in your "Future study recommendations" section and get on with your current research.

LITERATURE: STAY CURRENT

As in the previous section, there are no critical tasks in the testing stage in regard to the literature, either. Staying current with the latest articles in journals is a great habit to maintain. However, do not spend so much time in the literature that you neglect data-collection tasks. Allow yourself to focus on data collection and processing instead of reading because you only have one opportunity to collect data for this particular research problem. There will be time later to catch up on your general reading. Plus, you have already read an exhaustive amount of source material on your topic. A light periodic search for new on-point studies will suffice.

If you are conducting research that pulls data from other sources, though, you will obviously need to keep accessing the literature. But, your interaction with the literature will be different from the reading you did previously. Instead, it will be more like a dissection, slicing a source open and examining specific parts, skimming sources for a keyword and then recording the surrounding content. It is not the kind of literature-review reading referred to in the previous paragraph. Instead, it should be considered part of data collection.

ASSISTANCE: USING YOUR NETWORK

Hopefully, you have developed a strong network of peers and experts while working through the previous chapters because assistance comes in handy during the testing stage. If you have given assistance to others in the past, you will already appreciate how welcome and necessary help can be. Some help, such as extra hands to help with data collection, is predictable and part of the preparation you did in Chapter 5. Other help you will need during this stage is unpredictable and the result of the inevitable hiccups in the research process. After all, if outcomes were totally predictable, there would be no need to do research.

Data collection

Whether you need net holders to catch fish in a stream or counter clickers to record the number of times a kindergartner smiles during recess, it frequently helps to have assistants while collecting your data. Assistants must be trustworthy and accurate to be helpful because any mistakes they make will impact the accuracy of your data. The last thing you want is to have helpers who must be monitored so closely that you might as well have just collected the data yourself, especially if your data-collection procedure requires multiple people working in tandem. Who you ask assistance from will vary with the complexity of the task and the time required. Just remember that having assistants does not mean having someone collect all your data for you. You will eventually have to defend your methodology and its implementation. If you did not collect the data, you will not know how to answer these questions, which could lead to an unsuccessful thesis/dissertation defense.

Graduate students

Fellow graduate students will be able to help with more complex tasks because they have more experience with the data-collection techniques used in your discipline. Even if a particular graduate student is just starting out (as you were a few chapters ago), he or she has taken coursework and completed projects that have given him or her a foundation for understanding what you are trying to achieve, as well as the detrimental impact of doing a sloppy job. However, graduate students have less time to give because they are busy preparing for or conducting their own research. So, if your methodology requires frequent data-collection sessions, you will probably want to train undergraduates to help you instead.

Undergraduates

What undergraduates lack in experience, they often make up for in enthusiasm. Many undergraduate students are still searching for what they actually want to do with their degrees once they graduate. Providing opportunities to assist with research helps them explore one option, helps the university provide them with a quality education, and helps you get your research done. Although you will have to invest more time in training undergraduates to assist with your data collection, they will have more time to be trained and assist if they help you as an independent study project.

This will devote some of their coursework hours to you and will ensure a level of diligence from them, as they will be working toward a grade. If your data collection requires repeated measures or multiple collection dates, an undergraduate on independent study is probably the best way to go.

PROBLEM SOLVING

Some kind of data-collection hiccup is inevitable during your journey. Whether it is a lost text-based source, a data-collection location that becomes unavailable before you have finished collecting data, or a piece of equipment that malfunctions, the implementation of your methodology will not be as pristine as the proposal. Although assistance is available to help you work around these unexpected deviations, it is important that you think through potential solutions before accessing that help. Ask yourself the following questions before approaching your adviser or consultant:

- What, specifically, is the problem with my methodology?
- Will this problem impact the accuracy of my data? If so, how?
- What factors contributed/led to this problem?
- Will these factors be in play every time this methodology is used?
- Do I have enough time/resources to fix this problem and repeat my data collection? Is it even appropriate for me to do this?
- How would I revise the methodology to avoid this problem in related future studies?
- Has this problem negated my ability to use my proposed analytic method? If so, what are my options now?

Once you have successfully completed your thesis/dissertation, you will be expected to solve these kinds of problems independently, so it is in your best interest to foster that independence now.

Consult your adviser

Your adviser will have to approve any alterations you make to your methodology so it makes the most sense to work with him or her to resolve your data-related problems. Some alterations are necessary because without them, there will be no data to analyze. For instance, if your research problem focuses on the distribution of purple coneflowers along local roadways, you might have to change your study location if the highway you chose becomes slated for a construction project. Other alterations may be necessary if a portion of your planned data set later turns out to not fit your inclusion criteria. For instance, if your research involves historical references to the disappearance of Geoffrey Chaucer, you may have to throw out a particular article you planned to analyze if the journal in which it was published later retracts it because of falsified references. Presenting your adviser with the rationale for your proposed alterations and several potential solutions will speed up and justify the revision of your methodology.

However, other alterations may be seen by the academic community as an attempt to manipulate your findings. For example, you might be tempted to throw out the data collected from a particularly uncooperative child in a classroom behavior study because it does not seem to reflect the overall trend within the class. But, throwing this data out of your set could be construed as an attempt to only analyze data that supports your prediction, i.e. data manipulation. Most analytic methods have ways of dealing with outliers — data points on the extreme edges of the range — so it is best to leave this data in your set and discuss it. Incomplete data sets, where only partial information is collected on a particular research subject, are another problem you may encounter that is better dealt with in the analysis stage than altering the data set. Because you are just starting out with research, you may not have enough experience to make an accurate distinction between what is and is not data manipulation. Your adviser, as an experienced researcher, will be able to help you stay on the non-manipulated side of the data-collection line.

Others

If you currently use the services of a data consultant, you may want to schedule an appointment to review the early data you collect. This appointment will give the consultant an opportunity to review your method of recording and processing the data and highlight any weaknesses that could lead to the loss of information you will need during your analysis. You may also want to make an appointment prior to any appointments with your adviser if you are running into data-collection problems and are not sure how to answer the questions in the previous bullet list. If nothing else, keeping the data consultant apprised of the snags you run into will streamline his or her ability to help you during the analysis stage.

DATA: THE MAIN TASK OF THE TEST STAGE

The data portion of the Test stage is supremely important. Data are what this stage is all about. You will be recording information about your research subjects with the data-collection instruments you designed. You will be recording information about the circumstances surrounding the data-collection in your journal. You will also be processing this data into a usable form for later analysis. You may find that during your collection of the information you planned to collect, you run across unexpected information that may or may not be pertinent to your future analysis.

A good rule of thumb to use during this stage is, "When in doubt, write it down." Although you may not have a place for this information on your data-collection instrument, you can record it in your journal. These situations, musings, and questions will come in handy during the writing phase. Whether it is a potential explanation for an unexpected finding or a suggestion for future study, having extra information besides what is recorded on your data-collection instrument will make writing and defending your thesis/dissertation easier. It may also make it easier to focus during the collection stage because you will not have to worry about forgetting the information or worry about whether to record it. Instead, the information will be safe in your journal waiting for your next discussion with your adviser and leaving your mind free to concentrate on the main task: collecting the data.

Collection procedures

Before you collect your first datum, make sure you thoroughly understand your data-collection procedure. Changing your procedure midstream will cause analytic problems and essentially set up an unintended variable of "collection procedure." Instead, finalize all the details of your collection procedure before you begin so all your data will be collected in a consistent manner. Use these questions to see how well you know your methods:

1. Without looking at your proposal, try to write the procedure down in a step-by-step fashion.

2. If you cannot remember a step or get stuck, leave a space and move on.

3. Once you have written everything you can think of, pull out your proposal and check yourself. How close did you get to the approved procedure?

4. If you got stuck because the actual procedure for a portion of your methodology has not yet been determined, design a procedure and review it with your adviser.

5. When you have step-by-step instructions written for every facet of your data collection, save these procedures in your organization system.

You may want to type up a formal instructional document in case a committee member is curious or you need to train assistants. You definitely will want to review these instructions every time you collect data to make sure you consistently implement your procedures because consistency will make your analysis easier.

Training assistants

If other people help you collect data, training will be essential to the consistency mentioned before by making sure everyone is clear on the procedure and will implement it the same way. If the procedure only involves a few steps that are fairly simple — for example, asking people to fill out a questionnaire — training your assistants may only take twenty minutes immediately prior to the data-collection session. Promise to provide a snack for your assistants to lure them to your orientation on time and minimize any intimidation they may feel about the task they are about to complete.

If your procedure involves multiple complex steps with a high potential for variability in the way they are carried out, you will want to run a more formal training session prior to data collection. This session should be scheduled at least a day in advance of the first data-collection date to allow for questions and/or problems. If you wrote up step-by-step instructions in the previous section, use them as the focal point of your training session. When planning and running this training, be sure to:

- Schedule the training enough ahead of time to make attendance convenient.
- Choose a location for the training that is convenient for your assistants.
- Provide a copy of the relevant step-by-step procedures to each assistant.
- Verbally walk through each step while monitoring your assistants' reactions.
- Explain any steps that seem to confuse your assistants in everyday language, demonstrating if possible.
- Pause frequently to ask if anyone has questions.
- Encourage your assistants to bring their copies of the procedure with them to the data-collection session.
- Let your assistants know you will be at the data-collection location early in case they have any last-minute questions.
- If appropriate, let your assistants know how they may contact you during the data-collection session if they have questions or problems.
- Thank your assistants ahead of time for being on time to and courteous during the data-collection session.
- Be sure your assistants know how to return the data they collect to you, including an emergency procedure in case you cannot be reached when they need to leave.

Even if your assistants are earning independent study credit by helping you, it is important to treat them as people who are doing you a valuable service. The more gracious and appreciative you are, the better job they will try to do for you. This is not to say you should not correct them if they use an improper technique, but do so gently and in as positive and reassuring a manner as possible.

Visual aids

If an understanding of the rationale behind or possible outcomes of the procedure will help your assistants function independently during data collection, consider making visual aids for the training session. These visual aids might include Venn diagrams, flow charts, tables, and/or outlines. For instance, if questionnaires should only be passed out to people who fit a specific set of three criteria, you could construct a Venn diagram:

1. Draw three overlapping circles in a pyramidal arrangement.

2. Write one criterion in the space of one circle that is not overlapping with any other circle. Give it a code letter, and write it in parentheses in the circle. Repeat this until all the circles are assigned.

3. Where two circles overlap, write "[code letter 1] + [code letter 2] = no." Repeat this until all the two-circle overlap spaces are labeled.

4. In the center where all three circles overlap, write "[code letter 1] + [code letter 2] + [code letter 3] = yes."

5. You may shade or color this diagram as appropriate or desired. If this diagram will be taken to the data-collection location, consider laminating it or sliding it into a vinyl page protector.

As another example, if plants should be measured at a specific distance from the ground but there is anatomical diversity at that height, you could construct a flow chart that walks the assistant through the decision of whether the plant should be measured, as well as the choice of measurement technique:

1. At the top of a sheet of paper, draw a box that says, "Measure up the stem [distance] from the ground." Draw two (or more) arrows from the bottom of the box.

2.   Draw a layer of boxes under the arrows, and label each box with one anatomical possibility like "single stem" and "branched."

3.   Draw a third layer of boxes, and label them either with instructions or further criteria. For instance, the "single stem" box could lead to a box that says, "Do not measure," while the "branched box" could lead to two boxes that say, "Two branches" and "Three or more branches." Draw arrows between the boxes in layer 2 and their corresponding boxes in layer 3.

4.   Continue adding layers of boxes and arrows until all the possibilities an assistant might encounter have a measurement instruction attached.

Any visuals you use to train your assistants can be reused during your defense as slides to show while presenting your methodology. Presenting these during your defense will help the audience, including your committee members, understand how and why you collected the data with the method you chose.

Recordkeeping and backup

Recordkeeping and creating backup copies are crucial to a successful thesis/dissertation. It is too easy after a long collection session to shove your data sheets in your satchel and think, "I can enter those in the computer tomorrow." However, important papers have a way of disappearing. Original data cannot be recreated. If you lose your collected data, you will have to collect more to replace it. Depending on your methodology, this replacement could be costly, especially if it involves working with a completely different study population in a more distant location. You might also find it harder to convince people to serve as assistants if they know you lost the data that the last batch of assistants collected.

Similarly, avoid the temptation to put off recording your ancillary notes about the data-collection session. Potentially crucial details about weather patterns, stress level, light levels, delays, or other external factors will be lost if you do not write them down while they are fresh in your mind. If collecting the data sparked new questions or ideas, write these thoughts down the same day as well. Recording all this information right away will not only make it more accurate, but it will also free your mind for a more restful sleep. If there is some tidbit your mind knows you need to remember, it may play it over and over again throughout the night, causing insomnia or broken sleep — and the testing stage is not a time to be sleep deprived.

WRITTEN WORK: STAYING FOCUSED

Although you will not be writing vast sections of your thesis/dissertation during this stage, you *will* be writing. Note taking and data collection, as discussed before, are priority tasks that do require putting pen to paper — or fingers to keyboard. You may also want to review your previously written work, as in your proposal and other notes, whenever methodological questions arise. Refreshing your memory as to your rationale for various methodological choices will help you during situations that involve assistant training and problem solving. This, in turn, will help you make decisions that will stand up to scrutiny during your defense.

Data collection logbook

Previous sections have talked about a data-collection journal for storing notes surrounding the circumstances of data-collection sessions. A structured form of journaling this way is to keep a data-collection logbook. Journals can be written in any style on any kind of paper that is bound in any way. Logbooks, on the other hand, are designed to serve not only as an information storage solution but also as legal documents. If you are collecting sensitive data, researching in a competitive field, or developing an entirely new model, theory, or chemical process, then you will be best served journaling in a logbook. What makes a logbook special?

- Its pages are permanently bound in a manner that makes it impossible for pages to be lost or removed without being noticed. Additionally, numbering pages in ink is highly recommended.

- Every entry is written in a chronological sequence that is indicated with a time, date, and location. It may also include weather information, depending on the research location.

- Past entries are not corrected or revised. Instead, a notation is made to see the entry at another date where a correction or revision is written.

These logbooks may contain information surrounding the collection of data, thoughts and questions about the data, and possibly even the data itself. Making entries in ink whenever possible increases its effectiveness in any legal claims that might come up regarding authenticity of findings or originality of ideas because you cannot erase ink, and any corrections you make on the entry date will fit neatly into the space rather than being crammed in as though they have been squeezed in after later dates have been written.

Although it is possible to create time-stamped documents on the computer that will serve the same purpose, it is more difficult to take computers with you to off-campus locations. They are heavier than a small bound journal, need electricity, and are hard to read in bright sunlight. But, if you plan to have a laptop with you while recording data anyway, one option may be recording your log entries in word-processing documents, which you would then convert into time-stamped PDF files.

Thank you notes for participants and assistants

One optional writing task you may choose to take on is writing thank you notes to any assistants or human participants — or their gatekeepers/guardians — who took part in your data collection. Writing thank you notes by hand on real paper note cards is a disappearing tradition, which makes the gesture all the better. If you are hesitant about writing thank you cards or think you do not have the time, remember that blank cards come in small sizes, and you are only required to write below — or to the right of — the fold. Depending on the size of your handwriting, it may only take three sentences to fill up a 4.25-by-5.5-inch card. Just thank them for their time, tell them you appreciate their diligence, and let them know you would be happy to return the favor in the future. Remember that you are developing a professional network during every stage of your thesis/dissertation. You never know when a small investment of time on an optional gesture may pay off.

ORGANIZATION: TRACKING DATA

The length of this chapter does not do justice to the quantity of information you will amass — or have already amassed — during the Test stage. You have been using your organizational system for a while now, so you should already know where most of this information belongs. But, there are two new types of information you will have to track during this stage: data-collection schedules and data entry.

Scheduling data collection

Scheduling data-collection sessions requires more than just picking a date on the calendar. You will have to communicate with the people who oversee your study location and/or study population to make sure the session will occur at a convenient time for them. You will have to identify these convenient dates early enough to be able to coordinate them with your own availability and the schedules of your assistants. Closer to the scheduled dates, you will also have to coordinate training sessions and confirm that the sessions are on schedule. All these tasks require calendar and contact information, as well as phone and correspondence records. Keep these records up to date at all times in your organizational system so you can be on time to these sessions and even reschedule them in an emergency.

Data entry

How you enter and record your data depends on who will do the actual analysis and how they will perform that analysis. If a data consultant will perform the statistical portion of your analysis, he or she will have a preferred method of data delivery — most likely in a digital form that can be read by a computer software package. If you will perform the entire analysis yourself, however, consider using a simple spreadsheet for your data entry.

Even if you are taking a qualitative approach, using a spreadsheet to track details surrounding your keywords will help you identify patterns within the information you collect. *See the Organization section of Chapter 1 for basic instructions for using a spreadsheet.*

To set up a spreadsheet for data entry, label columns across the top of your file that correspond to subject-related categories, and use the rows for each data-collection instance. For example, in a qualitative study of references to women in news magazine articles from the 1920s, the instances might be each article researched and the categories might be article title, author, magazine title, year, and "term used for women." Once you are ready to analyze, you would then be able to sort your data by the "term used for women" column, which would give you a spatial way to see which terms were used most. You might even refine this sorting by adding a secondary criterion of "magazine" to see if there were particular magazines that tended to use more derogatory terms than others.

If you were doing a quantitative study on the same topic, you might break the "term used for women" category into specific terms like woman, girl, gal, dame, bird, honey, and "other/curse words." With the category split like this, you could record the number of times each term is used in each article and run statistical analyses on the data. If you have multiple categories split into multiple result classes, your spreadsheet will look less confusing by creating column subheaders, as well as headers. To do this:

1. In row 1, label the columns with header words — the main categories of your data entries. For any headers that will have subheaders, skip the appropriate number of columns before typing the next header. In the previous example with seven subheads, you would leave six columns blank before typing in another header.

2. In row 2, leave cells blank if they fall under categories that do not have result classes. For categories that do, type the first class as a subheader below its corresponding header. Continue

typing in one class per cell under the blank header cells. Repeat for each header that should have subheaders.

3. Back in row 1, make the header word span across all the subheader columns by merging cells. Click on the cell with the header word, then shift + click on the last cell above the appropriate subheaders. This selects the range of cells that will be merged.

4. In Microsoft Word, click on the "Merge and Center" button in the tool bar — it looks like a rectangle with an "a" flanked on either side by arrows. In OpenOffice, choose Format > Merge Cells, and then click on the "Align Center Horizontally" button — it looks like a series of long and short centered lines.

5. You should now have a long box with the header word centered over all the appropriate subheaders. You may format these headers at your will, using color fill effects, text effects, outlines, or anything else that will help you identify which classes belong to which categories.

All the pretty formatting in the world will not help you if you do not use the spreadsheet. It is imperative that you set up a routine schedule for data entry. Scheduling time for data entry on the same day as collection is ideal. But, if a same-day schedule is not practical, schedule a weekly data-entry date. Anything longer than weekly will leave you with an overwhelming task, one that has the potential to derail your thesis/dissertation because of missing data sheets or forgotten details.

Maintenance

Questionnaires, data sheets, flow charts, procedures, journal or logbook notes, contact information for your participants and/or assistants, and even the occasional news article may have crossed your desk at some point along your journey through this chapter. Where have you put it all? Hopefully, it is not still sitting on your desk in vulnerable stacks, or worse yet, shoved in a messenger bag waiting to be filed. Give special care to the storage of your original data and backup copies. Before moving on to the next chapter, make sure your organizational and disaster-recovery systems are completely up to date.

SUMMARY OF TASKS

Phase 1

- Periodically review the official wording of your research problem.
- Periodically search for new on-point studies.
- Type up data-collection instructions.
- Find data-collection assistants and train them (if applicable).
- Schedule data-collection sessions.

Phase 2

- Collect and record data.
- Record notes about the data collection sessions.
- Discuss data-collection difficulties with your adviser and data consultant.
- Write thank you notes for participants and assistants.

Chapter 7: Analyze

Now that you have tested your research problem by gathering information in response to your questions, it is time to analyze that information. Although the word "analysis" may be an intimidating one, it becomes less so when you think about the core purpose of this stage. Analysis is essentially taking a mass of individual facts and boiling them down to one or more statements that contribute to a discipline. This boiling process may involve statistics or not, depending on your methodology. Regardless, you will want to work closely with your data consultant — your adviser or a paid third party — to ensure the accuracy of your results and the legitimacy of your conclusions.

TOPIC: KEEP YOUR FOCUS

The bulk of the analytic methods you use should be outlined in your proposal. But, as mentioned in Chapter 6, things do not always go according to plan. If you had to make alterations to your data-collection methodology, you may also have to make changes to your analytic methodology. When working with your data consultant on these changes, it is important to keep your specific research problem at the forefront of these discussions. There are many tests and formulae you could apply to the data you have, but only a few of these options will actually boil this data down into a result that sheds light on your research problem.

Review your question/hypothesis

By now, you should be in the habit of reviewing the wording of your research problem — question or hypothesis. This review should continue during the analysis phase to ensure every thought and calculation contributes to the ultimate conclusion you will draw from your research. If you notice another pattern emerging that does not directly relate to your research problem, write it down in your notes as an idea for future research. Do not allow yourself to get sidetracked and potentially miss deadlines.

Revise your title if appropriate

As you near the completion of the Analysis stage, review the title of your proposal. Will it work as the title of your dissertation? If not, what kind of revision does your title need? Changes in verb tense or inferences about the findings may be called for. *Review the titles of the sample theses/dissertations you studied in Chapters 1 and 2 if you need a little extra help deciding how much revision your title may need.*

LITERATURE: PREPARE FOR THE NEXT STAGE

Time spent in the literature will be limited during this stage, but the interaction you do have with your sources will facilitate the next stage of your thesis/dissertation: the writing stage. The tasks in this section apply whether the literature serves as the foundation for your research or doubles as your data source. If you have limited time while working through this chapter, consider these tasks as side ones that can be done when you are not in the mood to engage in analytic tasks or when you are waiting for your data consultant to get back to you with information.

Organize sources by keyword and section

As you work through your analysis, revise the keyword lists you made in Chapter 3 so they include which section/chapter of your thesis/dissertation each source pertains to. The easiest way to do this is to add a column to your list in which you enter the name of the section/chapter for each source. You do not have to sit down and designate the placement of all your sources in one day. Just pull out — or open if they are electronic files — your keyword lists every time you refer to a source while making analytic decisions. If the source helps you carry out your methodology, then you will most likely need to refer to it in your final version of the methodology chapter. If the source corroborates the results you find, you will most likely need to refer to it in your results chapter. If the source helps you understand a pattern you see in your results, then you will most likely need to refer to it in your conclusions chapter. For keyword lists kept exclusively on paper, be sure to make these new column entries in pencil so they will be easy to edit if things change during the writing stage.

Find additional sources

As you analyze your data and try to make sense of what it tells you about your research problem, you may find you have gaps in the background knowledge base you are drawing from. If this is the case, you will definitely want to spend some time looking up additional sources:

- **To answer new questions.** You may need to find possible explanations for unexpected differences in groups thought to be the same, trends that oppose all the theories you had previously read, or a standard method that unexpectedly did not work for your subjects. These new questions will introduce a new set of keywords to search.

- **To support conclusions.** As you near the end of your analysis, you will draw conclusions from your data. These conclusions will be challenged during your defense to see if you can adequately back them up with data and support from the literature. It is important to look for supporting sources early while your brain is still in analysis mode so you do not get stuck with unsupportable conclusions at the end of your writing stage.

The sources you find during this additional search through the literature should be recorded in your notes and indexed by keyword along with your other sources. Share any major finds with your adviser to keep him or her on the same page.

ASSISTANCE: PROPER USE OF DATA

You will absolutely need some kind of assistance during the analysis stage of your thesis/dissertation. Whether that assistance comes in the form of running complex statistical calculations or merely checking the validity of your conclusions, at some point someone will need to evaluate your analysis and help you make course corrections if you are veering off track. The frequency and complexity of evaluation will depend on the complexity of your methodology and your demonstrated aptitude for analytic tasks during the previous stages of your research.

Clarify concerns with your adviser

While writing and defending your proposal, the expectations of your committee regarding your involvement in the analysis process should have been made clear. If you are not clear about which analytic tasks you must perform yourself and which ones you may farm out to others, make an appointment with your adviser to discuss where that boundary is. For example, you may be allowed to pay a consultant to run a multivariate analysis as long as you are the one that enters the data into the computer and develops the graphs that illustrate the results. Take detailed notes during this meeting, and refer to them every time you consider outsourcing an analytic task. Getting this clarification early will prevent you from embarrassing and potentially degree-threatening questions about who actually did your work.

Data consultant: arrive prepared

The expectations of your data consultant should have already been made clear while working on your proposal. If you have hired an outside data consultant, check your contract — or other service documentation — and review the tasks your consultant agreed to do and what you are responsible for providing to the consultant in preparation for those tasks. This will help you avoid wasting billable hours by ensuring you have everything ready before setting the consultant loose on your data.

If your data consultant is another faculty member (including your adviser), it is even more imperative to arrive prepared and organized to every meeting. Coming unprepared to a paid data consultation wastes money, but coming unprepared to an in-department consultation harms your reputation — a reputation the faculty in your department are supposed to glow about to future employers. These meetings should be scheduled at the faculty member's convenience to prepare and guide you through doing the entirety of the analysis yourself. An on-site data consultant might clarify procedures, check completed analyses for errors, and/or assist in problem solving. By demonstrating thoroughness, organization, and aptitude during these meetings, your faculty data consultant will feel his or her donated time is well spent and may later write recommendation letters for you.

DATA: MAKING IT MEANINGFUL

Data without analysis is just a collection of facts that will gather dust on a forgotten shelf. Analysis makes data meaningful and accessible, and allows you and others to use the knowledge to answer questions or make supportable conclusions. Although analysis can be time consuming, it does not need to be the frustrating and terrifying ordeal you have imagined. Just take things one step at a time, and ask for help when you need it. If you hit a low point, remind yourself that analyzing your data is the key to profiting from all the time and effort you have expended up to now.

Computer-assisted analysis

In this technologic age, researchers frequently enlist the aid of computer software while analyzing their data. This allows graduate students, who only have a few months to complete their analysis, to utilize complex calculations that used to take years by hand. If your data is not already in a spreadsheet or database, either by design or because of a lack of time, find a way to computerize your data now so your analysis process will be streamlined and easily backed up.

Qualitative data

The assistance computers can provide for the analysis of qualitative data has more to do with finding passages that need analysis than crunching numbers. With electronic journal archives, the bulk of your sources are probably in PDF or TXT format. This allows you to quickly find every instance within a source for a particular keyword, simply by selecting Edit > Find, and typing the search word in the box within Adobe Reader, Notepad, or other text document viewing applications. This is helpful if you have a specific quote in mind that you need to find in order to think correctly about a concept.

If you have important sources not in electronic format already, a scanner connected to a computer with optical character recognition (OCR) software installed will help you digitize your sources for personal use. If you have a scanner and a computer but do not have OCR software, an open source package called Tesseract is available from SourceForge (**www.sourceforge.net/projects/tesseract-ocr**). OCR allows your computer to decipher text contained within scanned images and stores this text in a new document. OCR is not foolproof. If the letters within the image are smudged or unevenly printed, odd words will result. OCR will also sometimes second-guess an unusual word that is not in the software's dictionary, changing it to a completely unrelated word. Although these imperfections can be frustrating, the ability to find keywords in a document without a magnifying glass and ruler is worth it. Be sure to destroy the scans and OCR files after your thesis/dissertation is approved and the final copy is filed, though, to make sure you are not guilty of any copyright infringements for reproducing the work in a new form.

Quantitative data

If you plan to analyze quantitative date in fairly standard ways — for instance, calculating means or correlations — you may do this in spreadsheet software. Tutorials for performing all the different calculations possible in spreadsheet software are outside the scope of this book. However, you may access step-by-step instructions through the software's Help features. For instance, in Microsoft Excel, select Help > Microsoft Excel Help to bring up a search box (normally in a right-hand column) where you can type in the name of the analysis you would like to run. OpenOffice Calc has a similar help feature, but after selecting Help > OpenOffice.org Help, you will have to click on the little binoculars icon on the Help screen to bring up the search box in which you can enter the statistical term you need. Both of these software packages have graphing/charting functionality as well, which will help you later in this chapter.

You may need a statistical software package for more complex analyses of quantitative data such as multivariate analyses. If you do not have a statistical software package already, you can download the free MYSTAT software package to run midlevel analyses and generate graphs. Means, percentiles, correlations, analysis of variance, and time series are just a few of the analyses this package can perform on your data. To install the package:

1. Go to the SYSTAT® website's product page (**www.systat.com/Products.aspx**).

2. Scroll down, and click on the "MYSTAT" button.

3. When prompted, choose to save the zipped folder.

4. You will then be asked to login or create an account. The account is free and immediate. The application only asks for contact information.

5. After you successfully save the folder, extract the files.

6. Open the unzipped folder, click on the MyStat12ENU32.exe file, and follow the on-screen installation instructions.

Once you have MYSTAT installed, run the program and look around. If the initial screen causes a momentary panic, open up one of your simpler data files inside the application. To do this:

1. Select File > Open > Data.

2. This will bring up a dialog box for you to choose your spreadsheet or database file.

3. If your data is in a Microsoft Excel file, click on the black triangle next to the dropdown box called "Files of type," and select Microsoft Excel from the list.

4. Navigate through the folders to the data file you would like to use, click on the file, and then select "Open."

5. Your data should appear in the spreadsheet-style window under a tab labeled Untitled.syz which should be re-saved with your data file name using File > Save As.

If you have an OpenOffice Calc document instead of Excel, open your document in Calc and save it as an Excel file before following the instructions above. If you have a Microsoft Access database, you can import the data using File > Data Capture instead. Do not be afraid to play around with your data in MYSTAT. Your original data file will not be harmed because it is saved under a different file name. Play around and see what you can figure out intuitively by selecting various items under the Data, Graph, and Analyze tabs. Search for items that match items outlined in your methodology. After you get your feet wet, work through some demos and tutorials under the Help tab.

Choices driven by your question/hypothesis

The ease of computer-assisted analysis carries with it the temptation to do many different kinds of analyses, not all of them appropriate. Not counting the playing around mentioned before while getting comfortable with software, double-check your motives for running a particular analytic test on your data, especially if it is not a test mentioned in your proposed methodology. The comparisons and trends you search for should be driven by your research problem and nothing else. All analytic methods carry with them a specific set of criteria that define which data sets are appropriate to be used and which are not. If you analyze your data with an inappropriate method, your results will not be valid, and you will face some uncomfortable questions from your adviser.

Hand-sketched graphs and tables

The construction of graphs and tables does more than visually communicate the results of your analysis. The construction process assists the actual analysis of the data as well. Choosing the type of graph or which factors to include in tables forces a researcher to think in-depth about the type of data available, what concepts they demonstrate, and which comparisons/groupings will best communicate these concepts. Sometimes the graph or table triggers new lines of thought that would not have been triggered without that visual input. For these reasons, the choice and design of visual data representations is a topic that might spawn heated debate between your adviser and yourself.

In *Writing and Presenting Your Thesis or Dissertation*, a free online guide (**www.learnerassociates.net/dissthes**), Dr. S. Joseph Levine of Michigan State University recommends sketching graphs and tables by hand at first. That way, you will not waste valuable time fiddling with office software on a visual representation concept that may get vetoed when you present it to your adviser. It is far better to put all your effort into nailing down the conceptual aspects of your graphs and tables, which may take multiple meetings with your adviser. Going through an exhausting cycle of formatting, then re-formatting, and then re-formatting again after every meeting will add stress to these discussions you do not need. Sketching the concepts allows you to be thoroughly prepared yet not invested in any particular graphic representation, so the positions you take during discussions stem from the data and not the nine hours you spent setting up the proposed graphs/tables. Statistical packages such as MYSTAT can make this process streamlined and effortless, but the sketching process ensures you know why you are generating the tables and graphs, thus preparing you for your defense.

Selection driven by your question/hypothesis

Bar graphs, scatter plots, stem and leaf plots, and Venn diagrams — your visual options for representing your data are endless. But, which ones are right for your thesis/dissertation? Work with your adviser or review notes from your departmental statistics course to make sure you understand what kinds of information the various graph types communicate best. For example, a bar graph would do an excellent job of comparing the total number of mantis egg cases per study site for three study sites. Although a bar graph might also compare these totals over time — with three-site clusters of bars across the x-axis — the visual bulk of this comparison might make it harder to comprehend than a line graph with three different colored lines to designate the three study sites.

To start the sketching process, ask yourself the following questions:
- How many study groups do I have, and what are they?
- What factors did I measure/record about these study groups?
- In order to make conclusions about my research problem, what kind of comparisons must I make between groups? Do I also need to make comparisons between factors?
- What kind of comparisons will my data support (i.e. simple trends, correlation, significant differences, or changes over time)?

If you make simple comparisons between two or three groups or factors, simple bar graphs, pie charts, or line graphs may serve you quite well. But, if you make complex multivariate comparisons, especially over time, you will need to choose more sophisticated graph types. A quick glance through your key sources should give you an idea of the graphing approaches at your disposal.

Key sources as formatting guides

Fortunately, you are not the first person to ever develop graphs and tables for meaningful communication about research findings. Just as you used the information from previous research to build your proposal, use the layouts and formats of the graphs and tables in that previous research as a guide to building your own. If your key sources used the x-axis on a line graph for time and the y-axis for the measurement of a trait, chances are good that the same setup will work for you. If your key sources include multiple subcolumns within columns of a table, ask yourself why they do and whether this applies to your own situation. When using your key sources as a guide, note how they differentiated between study groups and traits when placed on the same table or graph. You will need to use differentiation methods that translate in black and white for your thesis/ dissertation — such as dashed versus solid lines. Color, while making distinctions easier, will only be available for the types of media you can use during your defense.

Once you find a graph in one of your key sources that presents the same type of data analyzed in a similar method to yours:

1. Sketch its basic outline (creating an empty container).

2. Substitute the particulars with your own (fill the container with your variables).

3. Write out a sample caption to remind yourself what the sketch presents and why you tried this type.

4. Label your x- and y-axes, pie-chart slices, or other graphical landmarks if applicable.

5. Draw a rough prediction of what the data will look like on the graph. This does not mean you must plot specific points from your data, just a potential outcome. If you have trouble making one up, draw the same outcome as your model.

6. Ask yourself, "If my data plots like this when I generate this graph for real, what will it tell me?"

7.   Ask yourself, "Will this graph communicate the selected data effectively or does it obscure the point?"

8.   If it is effective, file the sketch for the next meeting with your adviser, and tackle another portion of your data.

9.   If it is not effective, try another graphing method.

This process can also be used with tables. When sketching, keep plenty of graph paper and a large eraser nearby. You might even want to purchase a dedicated quadrille-ruled notebook for this purpose to keep all your sketches together and easy to flip between. Do not be afraid of using a trial and error approach. These are sketches, a practice round. Making mistakes in this way is part of the learning process. Embrace it.

Flexibility and repetition

While working with your adviser to finalize the graphs and tables that will appear in your thesis/dissertation, the flexibility afforded by pencil sketches relieves anxiety and stress. If you have made a conceptual error, you may erase the error and fix it on the spot. If your adviser draws a completely new concept on a dry-erase board, you will already have a place to store a sketch of it to work with later. Try to focus in on one or two table styles and one to three graph styles. By using the same styles repeatedly, you will help your audience access your information. If you use twelve different kinds of graphs and three different kinds of tables, your audience will spend a lot of time trying to figure out how to read your visuals before they can even begin to read the content of your visuals. The focus should be the data, not a portfolio of clever presentation methods.

Once the types and formats of all your tables and graphs have been approved by your adviser, use a spreadsheet or statistical package to generate real versions for your data. Save the output under a name that includes keywords from the variables and factors represented — and be sure to save these files as JPEG image files for ease of use later. Study the generated graphs and tables. Are there any surprises?

Deviations from your original criteria

The methodology you developed in your proposal was developed as a plan. But, as you have probably found out, research does not always go according to plan. For every portion of your data collection that did not meet the criteria set forth in your proposal, you must now find ways to cope with these deviations during your analysis. Do not get overly anxious about this. Many people have found themselves in this position. There are methods of dealing with these data inconsistencies, also called data gremlins. Also, remind yourself that the whole reason researchers must actually do research, rather than just making educated suppositions, is because of this unpredictability. Your "imperfect" data still justifies all the time and effort you spend on your thesis/dissertation project.

Incomplete data sets

If your data sets include study subjects for which partial information was collected — for instance, you have behavioral and background data for a man but not his blood test results — you may be able to include the data you do have in some analyses and exclude the subject for other analyses. This kind of in/out will make changes to your sample size and complicate measures of confidence, so work closely with your data consultant to make sure you are not doing this exclusion in a way that will appear to be a manipulation of your results. If you have vast amounts of missing data — for instance, if a natural disaster wiped out your field site — you will probably not be able to handle this with statistics. Instead, you may have to plan a supplemental study that can be designed and carried out quickly to ensure your project is solid enough and complex enough to fill the requirements of your degree. This will be a discussion for you, your adviser, and the rest of your committee to have.

Unforeseen complications

If your data collection did not go according to plan in a major way — for instance, the school children you were set to study were recovering from a class-wide outbreak of the flu, which caused atypical behavioral issues — you will probably not be able to work around this with some clever statistics. Instead, analyze your data according to plan, and note the extenuating circumstances. These notes can be used in the discussion section of your thesis/dissertation along with a plan to repeat the study under more optimal conditions.

Post-collection wish list

Making a post-collection wish list is one of the easiest ways to deal with data gremlins. While you analyze your data, you may find you could have answered additional questions if you had one or two additional pieces of information or had just measured one more trait. If you find yourself in this position, it does not mean your planning was flawed. It just means you have an inquiring mind, which is a valuable trait in someone pursuing a graduate degree, especially if it is in preparation for a career in research. Recording this data wish list will give you a jump on the section of your thesis/dissertation that suggests future research problems or even follow-up research for yourself after you complete your degree and begin your career. Items to track on the wish list are:

- The factor, trait, or keyword you wish you had explored in greater detail.
- The measurement or scenario that would have produced the data you wish you had.
- The question that would have been answered if you had this information.
- The type of data you did collect that led you to this question.

Keeping this wish list in a spreadsheet will allow you to easily search and sort when the time comes to use these items. Even if you decided to keep it in a paper journal, however, recording and storing this information in your preferred format will save you valuable time during the writing stage of your thesis/dissertation, in preparation for your defense, and as you gear up to do research independently in the future.

WRITING WORK: MINOR TASKS

The written work required in this stage is fairly minor compared to what you will soon need to do in the Write stage. But, there are a few things you can do now to make your writing task more manageable later. Not only will taking care of these items shorten your to-do list, but they will also help your brain shift into writing mode, which, in turn, will make you more productive while composing the first draft of your thesis/dissertation.

Revised methodology section based on the proposal

If you were diligent in the writing of your proposal, then you have a head start on your thesis/dissertation. A little revision will quickly yield your first three sections/chapters. If your proposal was a less formal document, consider adding to it now so by the time you finish the Analyze stage, your first sections/chapters are complete. *See the Written Work section of Chapter 5 for guidance.* Once you have a working description of the research problem, review of the literature, and methodology in place, revise as follows:

- **Change the description to past tense.** In your proposal, the description served as a window into what you would like to study. Now that you have studied it, your entire thesis/dissertation will be a description of how things worked out and what you found. Your description of the research problem is the setup for it that essentially says, "I chose to investigate [research problem] because [description of the reason]."

- **Update to reflect the actual methodology used.** As discussed in the Data section of this chapter, your data collection probably did not go 100 percent according to plan. Research rarely does. Rework your proposed methodology so it uses past-tense verbs throughout. Then, work in descriptions of how your research was actually conducted where it deviated from the plan. While revising this section, think, "I planned to study [factor] by [method], but [x] happened so I [revised method by doing _____]."

By making these two revisions, you can now tell yourself — and others — that you have a working draft of your first three thesis sections or your first three dissertation chapters. Hopefully, this start will prevent intimidation or anxiety from hampering your productivity in the Write stage because you no longer have to start rolling the ball; you just have to maintain its momentum.

Captions for graphs and tables

Even though your graphs and tables are only hand-sketched at this point, it is not too early to begin writing captions for them. Wait until you are fairly certain you and your adviser have come to agreement about the information your visuals will convey, and then draft the captions, using the captions from your key sources as models. Even if your adviser later asks you to revise a visual you have already captioned, the practice you gained in writing the first caption will allow you to revise it with ease. The information needed for captions includes the graph/table style, analysis method used, description of the data presented, and the key finding being illustrated. These first-draft captions should be attached to their corresponding sketches by paperclips or staples. They may be hand written or typed, though typed drafts will be easier to revise and will get you one step closer to your finished thesis/dissertation.

List of key conclusions

After working with your data consultant to review your data, you should know some of the conclusions you have drawn from the data you collected. Some conclusions, such as, "I will never study anything involving caffeine and kindergartners again," are probably best stored in your journal and kept private — or at least only shared with fellow graduate students over the pool table. But, any conclusions that speak to the research problem should be recorded and used while writing the concluding section/chapter of your thesis/dissertation:

- List all of these problem-related conclusions in a word-processing document.
- Compose the list as quickly as you can, typing conclusions as they come to mind.
- Review your analyses and visuals; then, type in any conclusions you may have missed.
- Organize your list of conclusions in outline form. This will highlight major conclusions and show the group of minor conclusions that support them.

Once you have your initial outline of conclusions, review them for strength. Some of these conclusions may be more of a stretch than others. You might want to place a star next to conclusions that are strongly supported by your data and a question mark next to conclusions that are weakly supported. Show this list to your adviser because he or she may have thought of others to add. Your adviser may also disagree with you on your ranking of strong/weak support, so you will need to come to an agreement on it before writing your final draft in order to prevent difficult questions during your defense.

List of new questions

Throughout this book, you have been asked to write down "future study" ideas. These ideas have been from background information you looked for but could not find, methodologies that did not go according to plan, or interesting tangential research problems you found while scouring the literature. Now that you have completed the bulk of your analysis and your conclusions are beginning to take shape, you may find yourself asking new questions about your topic. Write these questions down.

If you now have more questions than you started with, rejoice. These questions from answers are the proof you have successfully digested the literature and your research results. You will no longer need help developing research problems because your mind is now developing them on its own, probably in quantities you will never be able to study in one lifetime.

Make a list of those questions that are a direct result of studying your research problem. Keep them in a safe location for inclusion in your thesis/dissertation, as well as preparation for your defense. Remember that you do not have to have answers to these questions in order to successfully write and defend your thesis/dissertation. Your asking of the questions is the key result your committee will look for.

Thank you notes to your data consultant

Once you have finished analyzing your data and know what conclusions you will write in your thesis/dissertation, take some time to write a thank you note to your data consultant. After all, without him/her, you might still be stuck looking at numbers or phrases and not know what to do with them. It does not have to be a long note. But, jotting a quick "Thank you for all your assistance and time" on one side of a 4-by-6-inch blank card in your own handwriting will go a long way toward developing goodwill for yourself, as well as future graduate students. If you hired the data consultant, consider writing this thank you note when payment for the analysis is due and slip the invoice and check inside. If a faculty member assisted you, resist the urge to deliver it via inter-office mail and splurge on a colorful stamp. This exercise, through its small details, is meant to demonstrate how much you value the help and support your data consultant gave you so give it your best effort. You will need the goodwill it generates during the next stage of the thesis/dissertation process.

ORGANIZATION: EXTERNAL LEADS TO INTERNAL

Organization is an important precursor to writing, no matter what document is going to be prepared. Organization of your research materials in preparation for writing your thesis/dissertation is no exception. At this stage in your research, you are immersed in your topic and are probably thinking along ten lines at the same time. Organizing your materials is an external way to begin the internal process of organizing your thoughts, so be thorough. It may save you from writer's block in the next phase.

Analysis output

Throughout the Analysis stage, you have produced new materials: spreadsheets, sketches of graphs and tables, computer-generated computations, and lists. Spreadsheets should be stored with your other electronic files and backed up on a regular schedule. Paper originals of approved sketches, complete with captions, should be stored in your binder after scanning them and saving the electronic copies in your disaster-recovery system. Your computer-generated computations should be in an electronic form that can be copied and backed up as well. Your lists should be saved as word-processing documents and stored with your electronic files, even if this means taking the time to transcribe hand-written lists. If you are a paper person, though, you may want to print out paper versions of all your analysis output and save them in a separate "analysis" tab in your binder. If a paper version of all your analysis documents would create a stack more than an inch thick, you may want to have a separate analysis binder with tabs for each of your major conclusions.

MAINTENANCE

Hopefully, you have developed a schedule and habit for finding new materials a home as you generate them. But, processing and filing tasks are not one-time events. You probably have pulled out previously filed items in order to generate more items to file. This accessing and re-filing will accelerate during the writing stage. Before moving on to the next chapter, make sure all your research notes, data, analysis output, sketches, and new literature sources are filed. Then, set a goal to re-file materials you access every night before you go to bed. The Write stage will require the repeated accessing of vast portions of this material, so do not risk losing anything to a less-than-optimal filing system.

CASE STUDY: DATA COLLECTION AND ANALYSIS NEED TO BE PROPERLY EXECUTED

Carl N. von Ende
Associate Professor, Department of Biological Sciences
Northern Illinois University
cvonende@niu.edu

BIOGRAPHY:

Dr. von Ende earned his bachelor's degree from Cornell University and his master's and his doctorate from University of Notre Dame. He has been a professor at Northern Illinois University (NIU) since 1975, serving as Graduate Adviser for the Department of Biological Sciences, as well as Interim Department Chair during his tenure at NIU. He also served as adviser to the author of this book.

DISSERTATION TITLE AND SYNOPSIS:

Organization of Bog Lake Zooplankton Communities: Factors Affecting the Distribution of Four Chaoborus Species (Diptera: Chaoboridae)

Chaoborus is an insect closely related to mosquitoes, but unlike mosquitoes, the juvenile larval stage of *Chaoborus* live in lakes/ponds and feed on small crustaceans (zooplankton). The study showed the distribution of four species of *Chaoborus* among a series of lakes in northern Wisconsin depended on whether fish were present in the lakes. One species was absent at the lakes with fish because they were prey to the fish, while the other *Chaoborus* species were absent at lakes without fish because the first *Chaoborus* species preyed on them.

FIRST-PERSON ACCOUNT:

Analyzing data is often viewed as the hardest part of the thesis/ dissertation process if you take the broad view that analyzing data includes interpreting and explaining the results of the experimental and statistical analysis. The relative difficulty of the two aspects of the analysis can depend on the complexity of the statistical analysis. I think both aspects can be difficult because students often are not prepared for the depth of knowledge and understanding of the data expected by the adviser and the committee.

The rewards of a well-designed and well-executed analysis presume that because you have done the hard work ahead of time by identifying the question to be asked, correctly designing the experiment(s) to answer the question(s), and selecting the appropriate statistical analyses, writing up and defending the results can be much more straightforward — perhaps rather cut and dried. However, although it is important to try to follow these steps, it is not always possible because sometimes unforeseen events interfere with your grand design.

I help students in all the steps outlined above, especially with difficult or more advanced statistical analyses. Before we have a discussion of each of the various stages, I tell them they have to propose initially how they would do it, and then we discuss the question, procedure, and so on. To avoid dependence in the case of statistical analyses, I make them do the analysis after we have discussed how to do it. Then, I check the results.

If I could give one tip to graduate students about how to write a successful thesis/dissertation, it is: Be prepared to leave a sufficient amount of time for writing and preparing the thesis. It will take longer than you think. Stick to it once you get started; otherwise, you will have to keep getting reacquainted with the data and analysis.

SUMMARY OF TASKS

Phase 1

- Periodically review the wording of the statement of your research problem.
- Revise your title as needed.
- Assign sources in keyword lists to the section/chapter of your thesis/dissertation to which they pertain.
- Clarify with your adviser and data consultant which analytic tasks you are responsible for.
- Digitize your data (if not already completed).
- Create an organizational plan for your analysis output.

Phase 2

- Analyze your data.
- Create hand-sketched graphs/tables, and discuss them with your adviser.
- Write captions for graphs/tables.
- Find additional sources as needed to understand/explain your analysis.
- Work with your adviser to overcome data gremlins.
- Revise the methodology to reflect actual events.
- Make a list of key conclusions.
- Make a list of new questions.
- Write a thank you note to your data consultant.

Chapter 8: Write

At last, the time is right for you to officially write your thesis/dissertation. If you have completed all the tasks from previous chapters, you will already have a head start on the document you will produce while working through this chapter. For instance, you should already have a strong draft of the description of your research problem and your methodology from the work you did in Chapters 5 and 7. This pre-Write stage work could make up a fifth of your thesis/dissertation draft so hopefully this knowledge will dispel any anxiety you may have about starting to write.

You will use most of the research material you have generated throughout your research journey during this stage so try to do the bulk of your writing in the place where you stored your material. All your binders and electronic files should be readily at hand at all times so your flow is not broken by having to stop and refer to a source. If you have family obligations such as young children or a sick parent, try to find alternate care arrangements on a regular basis during this stage so you can have some uninterrupted time to crank out words. So much of writing time is actually thinking time, so interruptions inhibit productivity in two ways: 1) by preventing your fingers from typing on the keys, and 2) by preventing your brain from processing the thoughts that must be translated into typed text. Hiring caretakers, making deals with a spouse or sibling, or even contracting out home and garden tasks during your writing time will be money well spent.

TOPIC: WRITING YOUR ABSTRACT

Though you will not be able to write the final version of an abstract until after you have a completed draft, try writing a first draft now. An abstract is essentially a summary of your research problem, methodology, and results that fit in a paragraph or two. In for-pay academic journal databases, abstracts are normally viewable for free and allow a reader to decide whether to buy copies of the articles. Abstracts are also helpful during catalog searches at the library because words from abstract text are used for electronic indexing and searching. Some abstracts do not accurately reflect the contents of the document. This can be frustrating, especially if the reader had to pay for access rather than viewing it as part of a library's subscription. To prevent this kind of disappointment and preserve your fledgling reputation, write your first abstract draft by stating:

- Your topic with appropriate keywords
- What your research set out to study about your topic (i.e. your research problem)
- How your research gathered information pertinent to your research problem
- Up to three strongly supported conclusions you drew from the information you gathered

If you cannot complete this exercise yet, do not worry. You will be able to by the time you complete your first thesis/dissertation draft. The attempt will get your mind flowing down the stream of logic needed to write your draft.

Revise and update your keyword list

Hopefully, you have been revising and updating your keyword list as you go. During some stages, you may have decided keywords were not pertinent to your study and placed them in an archive location. During other stages, you may have added keywords to help you discuss your findings. If these alterations are only stored in your head or informal jottings in a journal, take the time to make these alterations in your formal keyword spreadsheets as well. Be sure to include all the sources you have that fit under each new keyword, even if those sources are already listed under another keyword.

Review your question/hypothesis daily

Your research problem is the key to everything you have done on this thesis/dissertation journey. It is important to keep it at the forefront of your mind while you write so every statement you make, every logical progression of thought, and every illustration points toward your research problem. If you have not done so already, write out the official statement of your research problem in the same form (question or hypothesis) that you used in your approved proposal. Post it on your bathroom mirror, above your computer monitor, or even on the backside of your car's sun visor. Read it and reread it whenever you can to stay focused and primed for writing at all times.

LITERATURE: STICK TO WHAT YOU HAVE

Although your search through your discipline's literature is never officially over, the intensity of that search greatly decreases as you progress through the stages of your thesis/dissertation. During the Write stage, it is critical to stay focused on writing and not let your mind trick you into avoidance with one more trip to the library to read. You have already gathered more sources than you need. Extra reading at this stage has the potential to confuse and sidetrack you. Unless your adviser says you must read a particular source before going any farther, resist the urge to read and just get your writing done. However, this prohibition does not mean you have no literature-related tasks right now.

Update your literature review

One literature-related task you have is to update your literature review. Pull out the version you wrote for your proposal. If you did not have to write one for an informal thesis proposal, pull out whatever you did write as an introduction to your proposal. This section/chapter should already be written in past tense because it is describing research already completed. Check over the sources you covered. Are all of them still pertinent to your research? Are there new key and supporting sources that are not covered? Use your revised keyword lists for help in selecting sources to add to this review or to your introduction. Make sure this section/chapter accurately reflects all the background information you needed to conceive, design, conduct, and analyze your research. Diligently updating your literature review now will yield a complete draft of another section/chapter, as well as priming you for writing the sections/chapters you have yet to start by facilitating recall of sources you will want to cite.

Review the theses/dissertations you previously selected

Another literature-related task you have in the Write stage is to review the model theses/dissertations you selected in Chapter 2. This does not mean you must read these documents in detail again as you did when developing a thesis/dissertation style guide. Instead, read them quickly for:

- **Organization and focus.** Refresh your image of the finished document by looking at the number of sections/chapters used and how they are entitled. Remind yourself of how a successful document uses all its content to focus on the research problem.

- **Diction.** Refresh your mental "ear" for the kind of language and tone theses/dissertations in your discipline use. Although you have studied this in the past, you will more easily mimic diction the more recently you have read it.

You may want to make an outline of your own thesis/dissertation that mirrors the organization of your model documents while reviewing them. This will ensure you do not miss a section/chapter in your first draft and will likely add proper diction to your headers and main points. This outline does not have to be a detailed, five-level affair. But, setting up your section/chapter titles with subheads and a few bullet points underneath will give you a head start while your brain is already in an organization/ focus/diction mode.

ASSISTANCE: CONSULT WITH CAUTION

Try to work as independently as you can during this stage. The writing of your thesis/dissertation demonstrates that you are qualified for the degree you seek and that you deserve to be included in academia. The worst thing you could do right now is ask for so much help that you have no words of your own recorded in your final document. This inclusion of others' words passed off as your own is sometimes done purposefully, but you would not be reading this book if you were planning on tricking/paying someone else to write your thesis/dissertation for you. Instead, the thing you want to guard against is an unintentional, subconscious parroting of discussions you have about your research with other graduate students or committee members. Even in the world of academic diction, there is such a thing as voice. Your academic voice will differ from another person's, however slightly. Because your committee will probably know most of the academics you know, it would not be a good idea to slip into someone else's voice and be accused of not doing your own writing, or worse, your own thinking.

Adviser and committee

Although you should work independently, do not work in isolation. Make regular appointments with your adviser to look over your first draft as it takes shape. This will not only show your adviser you are making progress, but it will also give him or her a chance to steer you back on course if you begin to veer off track. Writing off topic, making faulty conclusions, or even writing in a nonacademic voice are all rookie errors that are easily fixed when caught early. But, if your adviser begins talking about new questions, remember that now is not the time to explore anything new. Gently propose that you add these new questions to "future study suggestions," and come up with a plausible reason why this new avenue is outside the scope of the original — and long-time approved — research problem.

When your adviser approves, consider distributing an early — second or third — draft of your thesis/dissertation to your committee members. This way, they can begin to orient themselves to your research well before your defense. They may have questions or concerns above and beyond those of your adviser that will need to be addressed before you distribute your defense version. Taking care of these initial revisions now in an informal setting will decrease the number of final revisions you will need to make post-defense. It will also cut down on the number of challenges you will have to face verbally during your defense.

Extra help for ESL students

If English is your second language and you have not yet joined a thesis/dissertation critique group, now would be an excellent time to join one. These peer critiques by graduate students at the same stage as yourself will be invaluable tools for polishing your thesis/dissertation prior to sharing it with your adviser. Keep in mind that as part of a critique group, you will be expected to give constructive feedback on others' papers. Do not worry if you are not strong in highly technical areas of grammar. Someone in the group will be. Just make sure you contribute to the group critiques somehow. You might be adept at catching areas of inconsistency or flagging places with confusing sentence structure. Do not assume you are failing to understand a passage because English is not your native tongue. Flag it and ask. Even if the passage is technically correct, the other graduate student may choose to revise so his or her exhausted committee members will not misinterpret it.

Spending time conducting group critiques will not only increase the proficiency of your written work, but it will also increase your proficiency with English as a whole. During these discussions, it is important to make sure all your remarks are directed at the work and not the writer. Rather than taking criticism of your work as a personal insult, do whatever it takes to receive the criticism as valuable assistance. The goal is to make written work better, not create an interpersonal hierarchy.

If your university does not have a critique group, it may have a thesis/dissertation support group where you could find someone with strong writing skills who would be willing to critique your writing for a per-page fee. You might also be able to find writing assistance from an on-campus writing center or an international student center. Critiques of academic papers take a great deal of time to conduct, so break the job into sections. This will give you critiqued and revised sections to present to your adviser at regular intervals. It will also give you a chance to switch the person critiquing your manuscript if the first person does not work out.

DATA: COMMUNICATING YOUR FINDINGS

After all the data collection and analysis you just completed, you know what your data is and what it says. You are the one spending the most time with it, so own the fact that you are the expert in this study. Even if you had a data consultant run portions of the analysis for you, you have been the one looking for the meaning behind the numbers and trends. Keeping your expert status in the forefront of your mind will alleviate some of the anxiety that accompanies the writing stage. Nothing halts writing progress like anxiety, and for many people, nothing produces anxiety like math-related tasks. Remember that you have already done all the collecting and analyzing; all that is left to do now is the communicating.

Key findings

During the Analysis stage, you made an outline of your findings. Retrieve that outline now and review it. Refreshing your memory on the findings you need to present before writing the bulk of your thesis/dissertation will facilitate composition. It also gives you one last chance to run questions past your adviser before launching. You do not want to get entire chapters written only to find out you will have to start from scratch because of a faulty premise or inaccurate understanding of analysis output.

- **Order of presentation.** Are you satisfied with the order in which you presented your findings in the outline? Is your adviser satisfied? Be sure the order you present your data and analysis will bring your audience through the progression of thought they will need to understand and concur with your conclusions.

- **Wording.** Did you write your outline in complete sentences? Did you use diction appropriate for theses/dissertations in your discipline? If the answer to either of these questions is 'no,' then take some time to revise your wording so you can lift sentences from the outline and drop them into your final document.

This outline of your findings is not the outline of your thesis/dissertation. You may be required to write multiple chapters, presenting findings from one outline section in one chapter and another outline section in another chapter. However, this outline may be re-used during your defense for the "Results and Conclusions" section of your presentation, depending on how your department expects defense presentations to be organized.

Computer-generated graphs and tables

Hopefully, you and your adviser have come to an agreement about the visual presentation of your data and analyses. If not, finalize your sketches before moving on. Take out your filed sketches and captions, and review the variables, factors, and potential output they are expected to convey. Computerized versions of your visuals should be done in such a way that they can be used both as figures in your thesis/dissertation document and as slides for your defense presentation. Generating graphs with spreadsheet software will produce output that can be easily embedded in word-processing software from the same company (for instance, Excel into Word, both from Microsoft). Saving MYSTAT graphs as JPEG files, which can be read by numerous software applications, will allow you to import or simply copy-paste graphs into word-processing documents and digital slideshows. Building your tables in a word-processing application will allow you to easily embed them in other word-processing documents of the same format along with their sister slideshow applications.

Software

Chances are you have already built tables within a word-processing program, so the following review will be brief. Pull out a hand-written table that you need to computerize, and open a new word-processing document. You will copy this table into your thesis/dissertation manuscript a little later. But, tables have a funny way of messing up the formatting of surrounding text so finalizing the layout of a table in a separate document — with the option of deleting and starting over, if need be — is a much less frustrating way to construct one.

1. In Microsoft Word and OpenOffice Writer, select Table > Insert > Table.

2. In the dialog box that pops up, choose how many rows and columns you need. Be sure to add a row and/or a column to house any headers.

3. Enter your headers and data in the appropriate cells so it looks like your sketched table.

4. Find a way with bold, borders, and/or shading options to set your header rows/columns apart visually.

5. Save this file with a name that indicates the figure number assigned to it and a keyword or two; for instance, "Figure6-Table-LeavesPerStem."

If you used MYSTAT in Chapter 7 to generate your graphs, check that you have a JPEG version of all your graphs before moving on. If you do not, take a moment to open up your output files in MYSTAT, and do a "Save as" procedure to make the conversion — the bottom dropdown box allows you to select a new file type. If JPEG is not listed as an option, look in the left-hand column for the particular graph you want to convert.

Double-click on its name, and it should bring up a new tab with just the graph. You should be able to save this stand-alone version of the graph as a JPEG.

If you used a spreadsheet, as suggested in Chapter 7, to generate your graphs, you should already have embeddable graphs ready for your thesis/dissertation. Simply click on the graph's tab within the spreadsheet, and then:

1.   Right-click on the graph so the entire image is selected.

2.   Select Edit > Copy in the spreadsheet program.

3.   Place your cursor in the appropriate place within your thesis/ dissertation word-processing file.

4.   Select Edit > Paste in the word-processing program.

You should now have a graph image embedded in your thesis/dissertation waiting for a figure label and a caption.

Finalized captions

Review your model theses/dissertations to see if their captions are placed just below their associated graph/table or on a facing page. If placed on a facing page, the formatting required is fairly simple. Merely type the text on a separate page in your word-processing document, and hit the enter key enough times above and below the text to center it vertically on the page. Begin the caption with "Figure [x]," where [x] is the number belonging to the visual. Check your models to see if the font for "Figure [x]" should be rendered in bold, italics, or both. The text of your caption, however, will likely be in standard font and single spaced.

If your models show the caption directly underneath a graph:

1.   Open the word-processing document you would like to embed the graph in. Place the cursor in the location you would like the graph to appear.

2. In Microsoft Word or OpenOffice Writer, select Insert > Picture > From File, and navigate to the JPEG version of your graph.

3. Click on the graph file, and select "Insert" or "Open." The graph should now appear as an image in your document.

4. To add a caption, right-click on the picture, and then select "Caption." Fill out the dialog box with the caption text and location.

5. Click "OK."

6. Your figure label and caption should now appear below your graph. If you do not like the way it is formatted, you may use the font formatting options just as if it were regular text.

If your models show text directly below tables, you may simply copy and paste the table into the appropriate place in your word-processing document and then type the text below the table. Be sure to format the figure label and caption the same way you formatted the graph's labels and captions.

Consistency is the main consideration here. If you have something formatted slightly out of step with preferences, it may not cause much bother if the formatting is consistent throughout the document. Even if you make a major faux pas and your adviser insists on corrections, with consistent formatting you will automatically know to make the corrections on every figure rather than having to study each one to figure out if it needs adjustment or not.

Privacy considerations

Review the privacy considerations you outlined in Chapter 4. If you have study subjects or locations that need protection from public attention, now is the time to make those alterations in your text. Before making these alterations, be sure you are totally finished with your analysis and know what your conclusions are. If you start using code names before you finish with your analysis, you may get yourself or your adviser confused during discussions or even mix up data sets. Your defense will be difficult enough without the gut-wrenching realization that you have mixed up your data and your conclusions might be flawed.

Keep a spreadsheet or paper list that records the real name for every fictitious one. Keep a printed copy of this record with your data so if your adviser or a committee member asks you a question about a particular data set, you can quickly find which data set to search for the answer. This list should also accompany you to your defense for the same reason.

Anonymity

Depending on your research design and study subjects, you may need to make your subjects anonymous before sharing data about them. Setting up fictitious names is one way, for example, in case-study research. Be sure the fictitious names do not sound too much like the real names so people will not be able to guess the real identities. Get a baby-naming book from the library or visit BabyNames^{SM} (**www.babynames.com**) if you are stuck for names that do not rhyme with the original and have a different syllable count. Be sure you have replaced every instance of the original name in your final document by doing a find-search:

- In your word-processing document, select Edit > Find or Edit > Find & Replace.
- Type in the original first name in the "Find" box. If you selected Find & Replace, you may also type the fictitious name in the "Replace" box.
- Select "Find Next." This should take you to the first mention of that name in your document. If this is a mention of the person you wish to make anonymous, click "Replace" or simply erase the name, and type in the fictitious one.
- Check around the name to see if a last name is used, and replace that as well.
- Repeat until the entire document has been checked, and then check the entire document once more.

If you need to make entire groups anonymous, consider creating group numbers or group letters. Be sure these group symbols will not be easily deciphered, such as using a teacher's initials as the code for his or her class.

Protection of research site

If your research site is private property or able to be damaged by too much public notice, consider describing the site in such a way as to protect it from interference. For instance, if you have been studying an endangered plant in a large state park, your research site should be described as "[name] State Park" rather than "in the meadow near the fork between [x] trail and [y] trail of [name] State Park." Otherwise, you may get many local college and high school students going out to "see" it, trampling it to death before it can set seed for the next year's population. Similarly, if you obtained permission to collect data on private property, chances are the owners will not take kindly to a flurry of new requests or flat-out trespassing. Describe these kinds of sites with enough detail to show why they were selected for your data collection but not with enough detail to allow hordes of admirers to ruin it for future researchers.

WRITTEN WORK: UNIFYING YOUR WRITING

You have outlines, lists, data, analyses, graphs, tables, and sources. Now, you get to collate all these items into a unified whole that contributes one new piece of information to your discipline. Intimidated? Hopefully after all the preparations you have made, you are not intimidated but rather looking forward to the challenge instead.

Complexity and length

After reviewing the model theses/dissertations during all your preparations, you should have a good idea of the expected complexity and length for your own document. Disciplines and departments vary, which is why your best guide is successful work from your own department. To get a feel for the difference between the two types of documents (thesis versus dissertation), some general guidelines follow.

Thesis

A thesis is normally 30 to 50 pages plus figures, front matter, and back matter. Ultimately, though, the fewest number of words needed to communicate the reason for and results of the research should determine the length. Content should demonstrate an understanding of the topic and the entire research process. It should be written in clear, concise, and logical language so the author can show his or her ability to engage in interdisciplinary discussions.

Dissertation

A dissertation is normally around 200 pages of material, but this number of pages can vary widely, depending on the subject of the paper. Like the thesis, however, the length truly is determined by effective communication of the reason for and results of the research. Brevity, even at this stage of scholarly writing, is desirable. Content should demonstrate an area of expertise within the topic and mastery of the entire research process. Since a dissertation will cover multiple facets of the research problem, organization and focus are the key to writing in a clear and concise way so readers — your adviser, committee, and the academic community as a whole — can follow your logic and concur with your conclusions. The document should set the stage for the author to engage in interdisciplinary discussions, as well as informative discussions with the public.

Style guidelines

As with your written proposal, you will want to use your department's preferred style while writing your thesis/dissertation. This style is not meant to override your natural writing voice, but it is meant to infuse your voice with an academic tone. It is also meant to allow readers to easily access your content because they will already understand the "rules" of the document and can focus all their energy on the content rather than the delivery. As a reminder, these rules involve:

- The function of the document
- Verb tense and tone
- Formatting
- Citations

Review the model you built in Chapter 2 from previous theses/dissertations. This is your primary guide. A secondary guide will be whichever professional style manual your department prefers. The tertiary guide for your thesis/dissertation will be your adviser's eye, so try not to depend too heavily on it.

Contents

When preparing to write the bulk of your thesis/dissertation, leave the possibility open for writing it nonsequentially. Some sections will come easier to you than others, especially those you drafted in the Proposal stage and revised in the Analysis stage. Take a bit of time now to make a rough outline of your thesis/dissertation using the headers, listed below, as your first level.

- **Title page.** This should include the title, subtitle, your name, your university, the date of the scheduled defense, and possibly your adviser's name. Check your model theses/dissertations for any additional text that may be required, such as a statement of why the document was prepared.

- **Signature page.** This is for your committee members to sign saying the document meets with their approval. Additional administrative blanks may be required as well. Check with your adviser for formatting and placement instructions if your model theses/dissertations do not handle signatures in a consistent manner.

- **Dedication and acknowledgements.** These may be on separate pages or combined. The dedication is optional, but the acknowledgements are an etiquette-must. Be sure to thank people who majorly contributed to your ability to write the document, including those involved with funding, labor, and family duties.

- **Lists.** These include a table of contents, a list of figures (graphs and tables), and any other summary of items that should be placed in the front of your text so others may access specific content easily.

- **Abstract.** This one-page summary presents your research problem and your major findings. *See the Topic section of this chapter.*

- **Research problem.** In a thesis, this may be combined with the literature review in a section called "Introduction." In a dissertation, this may be a chapter on its own. Either way, the research problem must be stated and clarified with enough support from the literature to demonstrate that studying this problem was worthwhile. It should also equip readers with enough background knowledge to understand the arguments made within the document.

- **Literature review.** As stated above, this may be combined with the research problem in a section called "Introduction." In a dissertation, this may be a chapter on its own. The literature review should familiarize the reader with pertinent sources of information that you used while conceptualizing, designing, conducting, and analyzing your research.

- **Methodology.** This description of how you conducted your research and analyzed your data should be detailed enough so others can replicate your study in a new location or with a new set of study subjects. Welcome replication; it is the method by which your findings may be generalized in the future.

- **Results.** In a thesis, this description of what you found may be contained within one section. In a dissertation, this may take several chapters, especially if multiple facets of a research problem were explored. This section should contain the tables and graphs you prepared, inserted behind the pages that reference them. These references should be labeled "Figure [x]," where the [x] is a number assigned sequentially in the order the figures are presented in the document.

- **Summary and conclusions.** This section wraps up the logical arguments made throughout the document and presents conclusions the researcher drew based on his or her analysis of the data. You will have to defend these conclusions, so beware of making unsupported conjectural leaps. This section is also where you may include the "suggestions for future research" that have been mentioned throughout this book.

- **Appendices.** If you have additional information needed to place your research into perspective or align it with the literature, consider developing appendix items. These can be reproductions of raw data, transcripts or notes from sources, detailed methodological instructions, a statement of position on a controversial topic, the critique of a key source, or any other piece of information that does not fit neatly in your regular chapters but is necessary to your thesis/dissertation nonetheless.

- **Sources.** This will be your bibliography or works cited section. Read carefully through your document for all citations, whether in the main text, footnotes, captions, or appendices. Use the preferred style guide to format this alphabetical listing of articles, books, lectures, and other sources. *See the bibliography-generation instructions in Chapter 5 if you stored your bibliographic data in a spreadsheet or database.*

Your university may use different words for the sections listed above. If so, use the ones your adviser will prefer. Also, the order of these sections may vary depending on your department's preference. Construct your outline accordingly. The important thing is to draft a functional outline so you can skip around from section to section, working on whichever section your mind is ready to tackle.

Once your outline is complete, it is time to write. Make sure to use proper citation techniques in every section/chapter because attempts to fill in missing citations later will place you in danger of unintentional plagiarism. Choose the composition medium that works best for you, be it paper or electronic. If you compose in a word-processing program, then revisions will be easy to make. If you compose on paper, composition may take place anywhere without the heat and whir of a hard drive, though you will have to be diligent about making copies and computerizing the text as soon as possible. The writing stage may take you weeks, or it may take you months. But, as long as the end result is a successfully defended thesis/dissertation within the university time limits, your rate of composition does not matter.

CASE STUDY: WRITING RIGHT

Linda Morales
Assistant Professor of
Computer Sciences
University of Houston at Clear Lake

BIOGRAPHY:

Linda Morales is an assistant professor of computer science at the University of Houston at Clear Lake. She received her doctorate in computer science from the University of Texas at Dallas. Her research interests include: the design and analysis of algorithms, security for networks and multicast groups, information security education, and ethics in computing and information security. She teaches courses in algorithms, data structures, and security. She has been involved in several funded research projects.

DISSERTATION TITLE AND SYNOPSIS:

Pancake Networks and Pancake Problems

This work used low-dilation embeddings to compare similarities between star and pancake networks and between binary hypercubes and pancake networks. In addition, a quadratic lower bound for the topswaps function is exhibited. This provides a nontrivial lower bound for a problem posed by J. H. Conway, D. E. Knuth, M. Gardner, and others. We describe an infinite family of permutations, each taking a linear number of steps for the topswops process to terminate and a chaining process that creates from them an infinite family of permutations, taking a quadratic number of steps to reach a fixed point with the identity permutation.

FIRST-PERSON ACCOUNT:

I encountered considerable personal difficulties that delayed my work by several months. The difficulties had to be resolved before I could finish my research and write the dissertation. The problems were such that it was not possible to devote time or mental focus to my work until the personal difficulties were resolved.

Once I was able to write the dissertation, I became aware of the challenges of communicating difficult concepts through the written word. This is not an easy skill to learn. Mastery of this skill requires practice, an intimate technical understanding of the topic, and an understanding of how to break the topic down into subtopics that can be grasped by readers. These skills are essential for writing articles in peer-reviewed journals.

One tip I have for graduate students is this: Before starting to write, clearly identify the main points you must communicate to the readers of the dissertation. Keep these main points in constant focus during the writing process.

Each main point will probably have to be broken down into subtopics in order to explain concepts clearly, and again, the writer should focus on clearly communicating the subtopics to the reader. The selection of topics and subtopics should be periodically reassessed to determine if they are appropriate and if the words are effectively communicating the concepts.

Finally, keep your writing style clean, focused, and simple. Keep your sentences short — no long or elaborate sentence constructions. And don't force the readers to have to look up lots of unusual words. Stick to common vocabulary, except when the nature of the topic requires specialized vocabulary. Particularly for scientific papers, you want your readers to focus on the scientific concepts in the paper and not make them have to parse difficult sentence structures or scratch their heads wondering what the subjects and predicates of your sentences are.

ORGANIZATION: STICK WITH THE ROUTINE

It is often tempting while writing to pull out stacks of reference material and leave loose sheets out in piles for quick and easy access. Resist this urge whenever possible to keep the risk of losing or ruining your papers at a minimum. Putting away the excess papers has another advantage: Physical movement can often jar new thoughts loose, so you may find these filing pauses make you more productive than had you stayed glued to your chair staring at your monitor.

Scheduling regular appearances

Because most of this writing will take place at your home, you may feel less inclined to commute to campus. But, regular appearances, though time consuming, will help you successfully navigate the writing stage. These appearances may include:

- Attending departmental seminars, which may give you ideas on how to present a complex thought.

- Meeting with your adviser to discuss your progress, which will give him or her a chance to point out revisions and things to avoid in sections yet to be written.

- Participating in a university's thesis/dissertation critique or support group, which will motivate you with short-term deadlines.

- Teaching or working if you have an assistantship, which will give you frequent, informal access to faculty when you have questions.

- Joining in on a weekly or semimonthly graduate student outing, which will give you a chance to blow off steam and help you have some sanity-retaining fun.

If you are writing your thesis/dissertation as part of a low-residency graduate program, these opportunities for visibility may not apply. You can, however, check in with your adviser on a regular basis and apprise him or her of your progress. The goal for this visibility is to allay any concerns your adviser may have about your ability to successfully complete your degree or the opposite and also to remind your adviser you still exist and will need his or her input soon for revisions and defense.

Tracking multiple drafts

Once you finish your whole document, or possibly distinct sections of it, you will be required to submit your work to your adviser for review. He or she will suggest revisions. Some of these revisions will be substantial; others will be minor. Make sure to view all revision requests as part of your training to be a successful participant in your discipline. In order to avoid confusion between the multiple drafts you will generate during this process, find a way to distinguish one draft from another. Whether with different colors of paper or different page footers, make sure the distinction is readily apparent so that as soon as your adviser (or committee member) pulls out the draft, you can tell which draft it is. If you do not do this, you may end up in arguments or circuitous discussions because of literally not being on the same page.

You might also consider tracking which drafts have been distributed to each member of your committee. This can be done electronically in a spreadsheet or simply on a piece of paper stored in your binder system. Number the drafts sequentially in the order they are presented to your adviser. This means your adviser will have every draft distributed to him or her, while other committee members may only see every third draft. Track both paper and electronic drafts you distribute. This way, you will have a record of the draft, person, and date in case of any disagreements or confusion during committee meetings.

MAINTENANCE

Before moving on to the next section, make sure your organization and disaster-recovery systems are up to date. As an extra precaution, make sure you have paper and electronic versions of your current drafts stored in multiple locations. Mail paper drafts to a grandparent. E-mail PDF drafts to a cousin. Load word-processing drafts onto a memory card or flash drive, and store them in a fireproof safe. Do whatever you have to do to ensure that, barring a nationwide nuclear attack, you will always have access to a current draft of your document.

SUMMARY OF TASKS

Phase 1

- Write the first draft of your abstract.
- Update your keyword lists.
- Review your question/hypothesis daily.
- Update your literature review.
- Update your outline of findings/conclusions.
- Outline your thesis/dissertation.
- Join a thesis/dissertation critique group or support group.
- Devise a way to differentiate between thesis/dissertation drafts.

Phase 2

- Write your thesis/dissertation.
- Meet with your adviser to revise your thesis/dissertation.
- Schedule regular on-campus or online appearances.
- Share your thesis/dissertation with your committee.
- Make computer-generated graphs and tables, including captions.
- Alter the text to deal with privacy considerations.

Chapter 9: Defend

Once your adviser approves a semifinal draft of your thesis, you can schedule your thesis/dissertation defense. The defense is your introduction to the peer-review process. This gives members of your academic community the opportunity to evaluate whether your research meets the requirements of your graduate degree program, draws supportable conclusions, and contributes to the knowledge base of your field. This will most likely be the most stressful stage of your thesis/dissertation journey because of anxiety while preparing and exertion while delivering and discussing. But, the skills you gain as you work through this stage will pay off, as you will be able to face demanding and potentially hostile people throughout your career by reminding yourself that if you survived your defense, you can survive anything. With the right mindset and preparation, you can successfully defend your thesis/dissertation with confidence and grace.

TOPIC: MEMORIZE

Throughout this book, you have reviewed the official statement of your research problem. Take the time during your defense preparations to completely memorize your question/hypothesis, as well as your thesis/dissertation title. The carefully chosen wording of both contains phrases and keywords you can fall back on during your defense. Whenever you feel the discussion may be veering off on a tangent that might lead to the committee asking questions you did not study, you can filter this discussion through your research problem and your title. Then, using these key phrases, you may attempt to diplomatically steer the discussion back to your study's focus.

LITERATURE: CHECK YOUR WORK

At this point, the sources used in your document should be set. Be it references within the methodology, sources summarized in the literature review, or your bibliography, there should no longer be any shuffling of sources. Taking sources out at this point could leave assertions unsupported. Adding sources could open up whole new avenues for discussion — discussion that will take additional preparation along potentially tangential lines. The only thing to be revising at this point is formatting and checking for omissions.

Review key sources

Unlike the source-revision mentioned before, reviewing the literature you have already cited in preparation for your oral defense will be well worth the time. Focus on your previously identified key sources, reading all the notes you took on them and even re-skimming the original abstracts, figures, and conclusions. These sources have been the backbone of your research, so the ability to quickly recall which source said what when answering your committee's questions will improve your credibility during the defense. Depending on how many key sources you have, you might want to relocate them — and their associated notes — to a small binder to have on-hand during your defense. That way, if a committee member questions your quotation of a key source, you can allow him/her to review the source while the meeting moves forward.

Search for last-minute major on-point studies

Although you will not include them in your written document, you might want to do one last search for highly applicable studies. For instance, an expert in the field might have just published a new article about the same process you are studying. Knowing that a recent study exists, familiarizing yourself with the abstract, or even reading the entire article, will help you if a committee member happens to say, "Did you see the recent article by [name] about [topic]?" It is more impressive to reply, "Yes, I was especially interested in [methodology or conclusion]," rather than, "No, I was too busy preparing for this defense."

ASSISTANCE: BEFORE THE DEFENSE

Your adviser will be at the defense to assist with the flow of the meeting as chair, but you will be on your own in the front of that room. Any help you need in order to defend your thesis/dissertation will need to be given prior to the meeting. This independent performance is necessary so your committee can assure itself that you have done the work, understand the academic process, and can effectively communicate with the academic community.

Recent graduates

If you developed a graduate student network, either by assisting more experienced graduate students or by attending social functions, you should know people who have recently graduated with the same degree you are seeking. Call, e-mail, or meet with a couple of these survivors to get an orientation on the psychological aspects of defending a thesis/dissertation. As you will probably find, a successful defense depends on more than knowledge and expertise. It depends on interpersonal skills, quick thinking, and the ability to remain calm. When you meet with recent alumni, ask for:

- **First-hand accounts.** Encourage them to tell you how the defense went from start to finish, including highs and lows. If you were at the defense, you might even have specific questions about how they felt during specific instances.

- **Insights and strategies.** Ask them to tell you what they learned from the process, how they would do things differently if they had to do it over, and what the key to their success was. You might also ask about any relational changes between themselves and their committee members after the defense, after the filing of the document, and after the graduation was complete.

Moral support

If you have friends or family who have supported your research endeavors, let them know you will need their support now more than ever. You will need people to hang out with when you need a break, to remind you that you are smart and capable, and to remind you of all you have invested so you are not tempted to quit. Be honest with these people about the expectations of the defense stage, and warn them you will most likely be distracted and/ or jittery during this time in order to prevent misunderstandings and hurt feelings. Come up with some strategies so they can support you without getting on your nerves. That way, you will get the help you need, and they can feel useful, ensuring that important relationships stay intact.

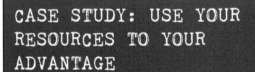

CASE STUDY: USE YOUR RESOURCES TO YOUR ADVANTAGE

S. Joseph Levine, Ph.D.
Professor Emeritus, Michigan State University, East Lansing, Michigan
levine@msu.edu
www.learnerassociates.net

BIOGRAPHY:

Dr. Levine is now retired from Michigan State University after 37 years on the faculty. His major areas of focus were Non-formal Education, Adult Learning, and Instructional Design/Technology. His responsibilities included serving as Director of the Non-formal Education Project in Indonesia, Coordinator of the Graduate Program in Adult and Continuing

Education, Coordinator of the Graduate Program in Extension Education, Coordinator of Instructional Development — Project for Handicapped Children, and Director of the Non-formal Education Institute. In addition to this administrative service, he also taught the following courses: Adult Learning Theory, Curriculum Development for Out of School Education, Instructional Technology, and Extension Education.

DISSERTATION TITLE AND SYNOPSIS:

Listeners' Preferences for the Rate of Presentation of Recorded Information (1974)

This work strove to establish that listeners have a rate at which they prefer to receive/listen to recorded information, in a manner similar to the way in which readers have a rate at which they prefer to receive/read written information. Such listener-rate preference was not measurable until the advent of speech compression technology, which was used as the technical base for the study.

FIRST-PERSON ACCOUNT:

This book's author asked me when I was called "Dr. Levine" for the first time and how I reacted. I was involved with in-service teacher training prior to completion of my doctorate and found many people most comfortable calling me Dr. Levine. I found it easiest to not correct them, as the focus of our reactions was not my title but substantive concerns.

Because my academic focus has been heavily tied to the andragogical view of teaching/learning (based on humanistic psychology), I have always encouraged my students to call me "Joe," rather than "Doctor." This has allowed me to provide a humanistic teaching model consistent with the content I teach. The more personal I can make my teaching and the more human I am with my learners, the greater the likelihood they will learn from me. Significant teaching can be greatly facilitated if it is based on a strong sense of relationship and reciprocity between teacher and learner.

As I began to approach retirement, I began to realize the significance and the power of the World Wide Web as a vehicle for sharing information. It was clear that such a vehicle would provide me with ongoing opportunities to continue to share my expertise as a retiree. In fact, the Web could provide me with a much greater reach than I had ever been able to achieve at the university. And, most importantly, I could do it with a minimal financial investment with no cost to the learners.

LearnerAssociates.net receives more than 3,000 hits each day. Never in my wildest dreams could I have imagined reaching a million learners in a year while working at the university.

One tip I have for graduate students about how to write a successful thesis/dissertation is to select an adviser and committee members who make the process collegial and not adversarial. Students often get caught up in politics that they have no control over — that have little relationship to their future. Through a collegial setting, they can enjoy the entire thesis/dissertation process as a learning process. It can serve as a model for their future professional relationships.

DATA: SIMPLE REVISIONS

Just as the Defend stage is not the time to make substantial changes to your cited literature, it is not the time to make major changes to your analysis and conclusions. Although some revision of the way you communicate your findings will be necessary, it should be limited to word choice and presentation order. If your adviser is asking for anything more substantial than that, ask him or her whether to reschedule your defense. You need to have enough time to collect your thoughts and trust your decisions. Doing a lot of content revision at this point undermines confidence and leads to timid presentations.

Review collection logbook

An excellent way to prepare for your defense is to skim through your data-collection logbook or journal. Looking at your collection instruments and reading through notes you took during the collection process will refresh your memory. Because the Analyze and Write stages are long and intense, you may have forgotten little details and enjoyable anecdotes that will add depth to the discussion of your research during the Defend stage. Although you do not have to build these items into your presentation outline, this review will give you access to them during the discussion portion of the meeting.

Review analysis rationale

Whether your data consultant was your adviser, another faculty member, or a paid consultant, pull out your notes from all the meetings you had regarding your analysis. Make sure you thoroughly understand the rationale for your chosen methodology and can summarize each major decision as follows:

- I chose [Method 1] because [reason].
- [Method 2] was an option; however, I did not choose it because [reason].
- Looking back, [Method 1] was/was not the right choice because [reason].

Even though people helped you make these decisions, it is important to discuss your analysis in first-person language because, ultimately, this is your research. If you find yourself continually using the pronoun "we" when verbally referring to your analysis, begin practicing the use of "I" right away. If you are really struggling with this pronoun switch, practice hand-writing your answers to the previous bullet points in order to embed the switch in your mind. If you do write these answers out, consider storing them in the back of your presentation binder so you have them if you need to center yourself during heavy questioning.

Select and prepare visual aids

After presenting a proposal and writing your thesis/dissertation, you should have plenty of practice preparing visual aids for public presentations of your research. *See the "Visual aids" section of Chapter 5 and the "Computer generated graphs and tables" section of Chapter 8 if you need a refresher on the types of aids at your disposal.* When preparing your visual aids, make sure to include:

- **Main points**, such as the title of your research, descriptions of your study subjects, the statement of your research problem, guiding questions, methodological steps, major findings, and conclusions. Remember to keep this text concise, and use a font size that is easily legible from the back of the room.

- **Graphs and tables**, such as the figures you used in your thesis/ dissertation and sample data-collection sheets. These should be constructed so you can zoom in on any portions your audience may ask to see in more detail.

- **Photographs and diagrams** that will help the audience connect visually with your methodology, such as photographs of your study site, labeled sketches of your data-collection tools, or flow charts of the participant-selection process.

Although you do not want to turn every word of your document into a slide or poster, you do want to have enough slides to maintain visual interest and facilitate understanding. Your committee members, already familiar with your research, will need something new to keep their minds fresh. Other audience members, potentially hearing this for the first time, will need a way to quickly access the information so they do not feel overwhelmed. Most of all, these visual aids will keep you on track during your presentation without having to constantly bend over your notes.

WRITTEN WORK: FILING YOUR COPY

During the Defend stage, your written-work tasks revolve more around sharing your work than producing it. The work you share prior to your defense will not be the final version because revisions will be discussed during the meeting. However, the work should at least be to a place that you and your adviser feel is solid, well organized, and worth the committee's time. This pre-defense sharing will be discussed in more detail in the Organization section of this chapter. All of the tasks in this section focus on the steps necessary to file your final, committee-approved copy with the university, the filing of which will complete the thesis/dissertation portion of your degree requirements.

Presentation and examination notes

Take notes during your presentation and record items that sparked a number of clarification questions. You will also want to track items your committee members challenged, as well as straight-up revision requests. If your defense will also contain an oral examination of your coursework, it might also be a good idea to jot down any topics you struggled to answer once your defense is over. That way, you will have the ability to improved upon those weak areas before you begin interviewing for jobs or promotions.

Revision

Once your defense is over, the committee will discuss the merits of your work in private. This will either be done by the committee chair excusing all noncommittee members (including yourself) from the room or by the committee retiring to another room. This discussion will have one of two outcomes: 1) You will pass your defense on the condition you make minor revisions to your document, or 2) you will fail your defense, usually with the ability to defend again after more extensive revision and study.

Consult with your adviser after the meeting to make sure you have recorded all the items that need revision and you get a time period in which the revisions must occur. If you passed your defense, the acceptance of your revised final version may be an informal process — essentially giving each committee member a copy (via e-mail, inter-office mail, or hand delivery) and asking for his or her approval. If you did not pass, your revisions will be reviewed as part of another formal meeting where minor revisions may yet be requested. Determination and perseverance will serve you well during this process. Just remind yourself of the reasons why you are pursuing your degree and tap in to your support networks if necessary.

Preparation

The copies of your thesis/dissertation that you distributed prior to your defense may have been PDF files attached to an e-mail or photocopies printed on cheap paper. Both are fine because of the number of drafts your document went through. But, the final copies of the final version need to be built for archiving. The guidelines below are generalized to give you an idea of the specifications to look for. Your university will have specific guidelines for its archival system, so look for more detailed specifications on its website or check with your adviser.

Paper copies

Paper copies will be expensive, but holding a physical representation of the past years of your life in your hands will be worth every penny. Even if your university uses an all-electronic archive system, make bound paper copies for your committee and yourself. Before making your trip to the local copy shop, make sure you have read the university specifications for:

- Paper composition (acid-free, percentage cotton, recycled, etc.)
- Paper weight (normally 20- or 25-pound bond)
- Paper color (white, cream, ivory, etc.)
- Cover composition (acid-free, percentage cotton, recycled, etc.)
- Cover weight (normally greater than 30-pound bond)
- Cover color (patterns, texture prohibitions, hue preferences, etc.)
- Binding type (comb bound, perfect bound, tape bound, etc.)

These specifications are important to the university's ability to make the knowledge you added to your field available to academia for generations, so follow them closely. You will enjoy the feel of an archival document. It will look as sharp as your mind, and the construction of it will allow you to flip through your masterpiece for years to come without looking bedraggled.

Electronic copies

Electronic copies are inexpensive — or free — and use fewer resources, but they are less satisfying on the psychological "look what I just did" front. But, as more universities are moving to an electronic workflow, you will probably be asked to submit an electronic version of your thesis/dissertation alone or in addition to paper copies. Check your university's specifications for the following elements before converting your word processing file:

- File type (.pdf, .epub, .txt, etc.)
- Number of files (all information in one, separate files for figures, etc.)
- File naming conventions (a special format that may include your last name, keyword, adviser, year, etc.)
- Font (restrictions on style, restrictions on size, mandatory embedding, etc.)
- Security protocols (encryption, login credentials, software preferences, etc.)
- Size (limits and methods of making large files fit within the limits)

These specifications are designed to ensure your files will not be corrupted and will be transferable as new electronic file formats become standard. Submitting a version of your thesis/dissertation to an electronic archive will also increase the likelihood that other researchers will be able to use your contribution in their studies and expand the knowledge base about your topic even further.

Distribution

By this time, you will already be familiar with your committee members' preferences for document delivery. Be gracious, and thank your committee members for their time when you deliver your final copies to them, no matter what the tone of your defense was. If you are at the point of distributing your finished thesis/dissertation and have passed your defense, you are now a colleague of these faculty members. Whether they were hostile or supportive, they judged your work on its merits and approved its inclusion in your field's knowledge base.

But, distributing final copies to your committee is not enough. You must distribute signed copies to the university as well. Be aware that administrative offices, e-mail addresses, and databases change, so make sure you check the university's distribution instructions for your final copies before sending them off. These instructions should include:

- Signature requirements
- Quantity of copies to be filed
- Locations for paper copy delivery
- URL or e-mail address for electronic copy delivery
- Descriptions of the administrative confirmation that the copies were received, so you know what to look for
- Contact information in case your copies were sent but not received
- Deadlines for filing in relation to your defense and graduation dates
- Filing fees and how to pay them

This may seem like proverbial red tape, but your work bears the name of the university. The quality of your thesis/dissertation reflects not only on you and your adviser but also on the university as a whole. The university invested its resources in your education, only a portion of which were covered by your tuition. When you work through the above requirements, try to look at your relationship with the university as a partnership rather than a dictatorship. After all, they get to use your work to demonstrate the quality of the education they provide (attracting new students and donors), and you get to use their name when applying for future positions.

ORGANIZATION: SCHEDULING AND PREPARING FOR YOUR DEFENSE

As soon as your adviser says your thesis/dissertation is ready to defend (or will be ready in the near future), schedule your defense. Scheduling should be done quickly because faculty calendars fill up quickly. Get multiple dates so you can build a backup plan if something goes wrong. Also, if you aim to graduate in a particular semester, make sure these defense dates are within the administrative schedule for that semester. For instance, if you wanted to graduate in the spring and commencement is on May 15, you will not want to schedule your defense on May 7. Try to schedule your defense a month or two in advance, and then check in with your committee two to three weeks ahead of the meeting to make sure everyone is still planning to attend.

Technically, this entire chapter covers tasks that will prepare you for your defense. But, the following items are specifically geared toward making you as comfortable as possible during the defense. Although it is not possible to prevent every misunderstanding and forgotten fact, it is possible to cut down on the number of times you feel like crawling under the lectern.

Meeting with your adviser to make sure you are in sync

As chair of your committee, your adviser will be in charge of the agenda during your defense. He or she will also be the one monitoring the tone and keeping things moving in a productive direction. You will be in a much better position if you meet before your defense to make sure you both have the same perspectives on your research. Having similar ideas about the strengths and weaknesses of your study will give you some confidence that at least one person in the room agrees with your assessment. If you and your adviser do not agree on these perspectives, you will have the added worry of being caught off-guard by questions from the one person on the committee who should give you the most support. Even if you and your adviser will never agree on these points, it is important to be aware of and plan for these disagreements so you can calmly field these questions without feeling betrayed.

Submitting your thesis/dissertation in advance

Show your respect for your committee's time by submitting the defense version of your thesis/dissertation to members with enough time for them to study it. If you give them a 100-page document one week before your defense, chances are they will not have enough time to digest it and then slow the meeting down with questions that would have been answered with a thorough read. The rest of your committee members are not as familiar with the work as your adviser, so allow them enough time to get oriented and start thinking critically.

This advance distribution does leave the possibility of lost drafts, however. If you know that one of your committee members is notorious for losing papers, check in with all your committee members via e-mail to make sure they all have their drafts, and ask if there are any initial questions you can answer prior to the defense. This way, you are not singling out the notorious committee member. This will also demonstrate your willingness to participate in the discussion that is to come, which should assure your committee members that you are indeed ready to have this discussion.

Thesis defense coursework review

If you are defending a thesis as part of a master's degree program that requires an oral examination covering your coursework, your defense preparation will not be solely focused on your thesis. In order to prepare for this coursework review, look over the notes from all your classes. Pay particular attention to core courses, as well as those taught by your committee members. Any concept from any course you took is fair game, but you will most likely be asked a series of questions that will increase in complexity as the examination moves on. Although a detailed study plan for this is outside the scope of this book, one tip is to look over your course notes and remind yourself that you are not expected to know every detail. You are not required to answer 100 percent of the questions correctly in order to pass, but you are expected to be able to describe and discuss major concepts.

Organizing your materials for the defense

As much as you might be tempted, do not try to bring every note, source, and data sheet to your defense. Bringing everything with you would be a logistical nightmare, requiring exertion of energy that would be better spent answering questions. Planning to bring everything with you might also weaken your resolve to thoroughly prepare because you could continually fall back on "I will just look that up" when you reach portions of your research you feel less comfortable with. Too many "look-ups" will break the flow of your presentation and lessen your committee's confidence that you are ready to join the academic peerage.

This is not to say you cannot bring anything with you. A reasonable packing list includes:

- **Printed copy of thesis/dissertation**, three-hole punched and stored in a binder. This should be the exact version you have distributed to your committee. It should be printed one-sided so you can write revision notes on the blank backsides to the left of the associated text on the right-hand pages.

- **Notes** you write in preparation for the presentation, including an outline and potential answers to analysis questions. These should be three-hole punched and stored in the same binder with your thesis/dissertation, separated with a tabbed divider. Make sure the font size and size of your writing is large enough that you will easily be able to read it despite quick glances and a nervous mind.

- **Key sources**, including their associated notes. These should be stored in a separate small binder so they may be handed to a curious committee member if necessary.

- **Visual aids** you prepared to illustrate your points. *See the Organization section of Chapter 5 for a full list of visual presentation utilities and methods you may choose.* Make sure to store these visual aids in a container — binder, portable file box, etc. — that will keep them easily accessible and organized.

- **Note-taking and demonstration materials** such as pens, highlighters, sticky-flags, and any show-and-tell items from your methodology that could be passed around the room. These could be packed in your regular satchel, in a portable file box, or any other container with a handle or strap.

These items should be gathered and organized three to five days ahead of your defense. The sooner you have them set, the more time you will have to practice your presentation. As with your proposal, have planned backup methods for presenting your thesis/dissertation research. *See the Organization section of Chapter 5 to make sure you have the tools in place to present on time in the face of technical difficulties or packing mishaps.* If the alumni whom you talked to suggested bringing other items along, by all means, add them to the list. The important thing is to walk in more dependent on your brain than a stack of papers.

Organizing yourself for the defense

In order to successfully navigate your defense, you will need to have your mind organized, as well as, or better than, your materials. Defending your thesis/dissertation will take clarity to answer questions, patience to handle challenges from your committee, and open-minded determination to accept revision requests. The following strategies should get you as ready as you can be through preparation — meaning no last-minute cramming.

Practicing your presentation

If you work according to schedule, you will have your presentation materials together with at least three days left before the defense. Use these days to practice your delivery. How you practice depends on your speaking style. If the way you practiced for your proposal worked well for you, repeat it. *If not, see the Organization section of Chapter 5 for a different approach to try.* It is important to practice out loud so you can time yourself and figure out if you can actually flesh out the points of your outline. Rehearsing out loud also gives you the ability to practice using your visual aids in real time. If you run into rough spots or technical mishaps, find solutions to these problems, and make notations at the appropriate place in your notes or draft. Practicing out loud tends to make people feel self-conscious, but by conquering that anxiety, you will be one step closer to handling yourself well in front of your committee.

Make sure to rehearse at least once a day for three days so your delivery feels natural and your mind has time to absorb what you learn during each rehearsal. Waiting to practice over and over the night before your defense has the potential to feed your nervousness rather than dispel it. You need time in between rehearsals to solve problems and allow your mind to create better ways of stating things. This subconscious process often takes the performance of another unrelated task, such as driving the car or washing dishes. If you have diligently practiced, do not feel guilty about taking these physical-activity breaks. They will end up being some of the best preparation you did.

Getting yourself in the right frame of mind

The process of designing, conducting, analyzing, writing, and defending a thesis/dissertation is not an easy one. It involves one person — you — trying to accomplish something under the guidance of a group of people — your committee. Everyone involved has different personalities, tendencies, and preferences. Whether you have gotten along with your committee or have struggled with personality conflicts the entire time, now is the time to separate emotion from the academic process. The defense is the closest thing to an objective test of your research skills the committee has.

Every faculty member on every committee has been charged with the duty to evaluate the readiness of degree candidates to take the professional step. Although individual faculty members carry out this duty in many different ways, not all of them with objectivity, it is your duty to view every question and remark as having a noble intent rather than a malicious one. Paranoia, pride, and holding grudges are the fastest means by which to get into an argument during your defense. Take the moral high ground at all times, and choose the most professional response you can to anything that seems hostile to you. Stress skews perception, so avoid overreaction by assuming intentions are good. Save the venting for afterward. Even if a committee member makes a remark with hostile intent, your failure to take the bait will make you the ultimate winner.

Relaxing and getting some sleep

If you have practiced your presentation enough ahead of time, reward yourself with a relaxing activity and a full night's sleep. See a movie with your spouse. Take your kids to the arcade. Read a fun book in the bathtub. Do not be afraid to disconnect your mind from the stressful task ahead. You have worked toward this day for years, so allow yourself to accept you are ready. Laughter is a great stress reliever, so find ways to make sure you get a good dose the night before your defense. Not only will it relax you, but it will also probably help you sleep — and sleep is what you need most so you can face the big day refreshed and with a clear mind.

Recruiting a chauffeur

Hopefully, you have a supportive family member or friend who is willing to be a friendly face in the crowd. But, if no one can attend your entire defense, recruit someone to drive you home afterward. Find someone who is flexible about times and does not mind nonstop chatter or silence. The exertion of standing in front of an audience for up to four hours, the mental toll of all the work you have done for years, and the stress relief of the worst being over will affect you in unpredictable ways. Some people cry, others shake, and still others get a euphoric high. None of these states is conducive to safe driving. No matter what you choose to do after your defense, be sure to make arrangements that reward you for a job well done and allow you to stop thinking completely. Just make sure that before you stop thinking, either on- or off-campus, you remember to thank your committee members for their assistance with a smile and a firm handshake.

Defending your thesis/dissertation

You have rehearsed. You have slept. Now is the time to perform. According to *Webster's New World Dictionary*, the word "perform" has three definitions, all of which apply to your defense. The first is to bring something to completion. The second is to meet requirements. The third is to give a performance, as in a dramatic role. Successfully defending your thesis/ dissertation brings your research to completion by bringing it through the peer-review process — the final stamp of approval for any scholarly work. A successful defense is also a requirement for earning your graduate degree. These two facets are fairly straightforward, but you may be asking, "How does the dramatic performance angle factor in, and how will it help me accomplish the other two?"

Adviser as master of ceremonies

If you picture your adviser as your defense's master of ceremonies, this will help you understand the tasks he or she is in charge of. Your adviser will call the meeting to order with a short introduction, not unlike the person who walks on stage first before a variety show and communicates the order of events so the audience's expectations are set properly. Your adviser will introduce the members of the committee to the audience if there are any spectators in the room. He or she also controls the microphone, dictating who has the right to speak and when. If you need a stress-relieving image, just think of your adviser as the one in the purple-sequined tux jacket saying, "Ladies and gentlemen!"

Committee as stage managers

If you picture your committee members as your defense's stage managers, this will help you understand the motive behind the direction they give you. They, like stage managers at a variety show, are in charge of getting you and the findings from your research in the right place at the right time. Last-minute changes in modes of presentation, challenges when you are headed in the wrong direction, and reminders of which mark you are aiming for — the duties your committee performs — are a backstage effort to get your work in the kind of shape that will yield cheers rather than jeers. This kind of instruction can be delivered in a gruff, matter-of-fact manner at times, but try not to take it to heart and separate the performance from yourself as an individual.

You as headliner

Because it is your defense, you are the headliner — the main attraction. This does not mean you will be the only one on stage. Your committee members will make guest appearances by asking questions and suggesting revisions, but ultimately, you are the one everyone is there to see. Your defense will potentially be the only time you will be able to talk about your research to a captive audience, an audience that must stay put until you cover every facet. This is one reason why it is best if you are passionate about your topic. You will be more animated, convincing, and infectious with enthusiasm if your performance involves the description of an experience you loved.

Even if your topic was one of convenience, it is important to put on a good show. Part of this is to look presentable; wear comfortable clothing that looks professional and demonstrates respect for the audience rather than sloppy or ostentatious outfits. Use as many sensory channels as you can during your performance to keep everyone engaged. This does not mean you have to juggle flaming rings. Delivering a presentation that includes visual aids and a few pass-around demonstration items should do it. The important thing is to break the monotony of the mostly auditory input to keep your own mind engaged in your content delivery and to keep your audience — including your committee — attentive while receiving your content.

Working the room

Part of being a good performer is the ability to work a room. This includes making eye contact that feels natural, using subtle hand gestures, speaking with an appropriate volume and speed, and pausing in well-timed places to allow the listener's mind to catch up with the ears. If you have friendly faces in the crowd, you may find yourself gravitating toward them more than others. However, it is important to make everyone in the room feel as though you are speaking to them, so try to go to the friendly faces when you need reassurance, but look at everyone else for most of your presentation. During the question period, the bulk of your eye contact can be with the person who asked the question, but try to draw others in to the conversation by looking around the room as well.

If you are the one controlling your slides and other visual aids, you will have gestures built in to your presentation already. Pointing to items on your slides, picking up demonstration items, and even turning note pages will help your hands be productive and moving without fidgeting. If you find your hands sweating and shaking, consider picking up a pen, dry erase marker, or any other writing instrument you might use at some point in the presentation. You can shift this instrument from hand to hand, press your thumb on the cap, or even write with it when you need to get your fidgets out. Keep your hands out of your pockets if you can to avoid pulling your clothes into unappealing shapes or appearing disinterested.

If you tend to speak too fast, too slow, too loud, or too quiet when speaking in front of a crowd, consider having someone in the audience give you subtle signals so you can make adjustments. If these signals will be too distracting, try to self-monitor by watching your committee members for signs that your message may not be getting through. Watch for signs of discomfort, and make your best guess as to how you can alter your delivery to help them sit back and enjoy.

Pausing to allow for receptive processing can look a little odd if you just suddenly stop talking. Make these pauses natural by taking a sip of water, turning a page of your notes in a deliberate manner, walking over to the screen to point out a specific point, asking if anyone has questions before moving on, or taking a moment to breathe. The number of pauses to take depends on how long your presentation will be and the complexity of the content being presented. Just choose moments at which you need to pause and gather your thoughts before moving on. Chances are these moments will be the same for your audience.

When you have finished with your presentation, make sure to thank everyone for listening, and invite questions. After a few questions have been asked and answered, your adviser will typically then direct this portion a little more purposefully. You will be reacting rather than driving during the rest of your time in the spotlight. Do the best you can to continue engaging the audience with the methods you used during your presentation. At all times, be professional and courteous, even if you feel provoked. There will be more appropriate venues to iron out disagreements; this venue is all about passing your defense, meeting a requirement, getting the signatures, and earning that degree. Stay focused, and you will succeed.

SUMMARY OF TASKS

Phase 1

- Memorize the statement of your research problem and your title.
- Review your key sources.
- Search for last-minute on-point studies.
- Review your data-collection logbook.
- Review your analysis rationale.
- Ask recent graduates for tips and anecdotes.
- Schedule your defense.
- Find people to provide moral support.
- Find a post-defense chauffeur.
- Meet with your adviser to confirm positions on your research.
- Distribute the defense version of your thesis/dissertation.

Phase 2

- Select and prepare visual aids.
- Confirm your defense date with your committee.
- Outline and prepare notes for your presentation.
- Practice your presentation.
- Organize and pack the materials for your defense.
- Defend your thesis/dissertation.
- Revise your thesis/dissertation.
- Get the required signatures for your thesis/dissertation.
- File the final version of your thesis/dissertation with your committee and the university.

Chapter 10: Share

"It isn't finished until it's published."
—*Dr. Samuel M. Scheiner, Ph.D., to a Ph.D. candidate
at her post-defense reception*

You have defended your thesis/dissertation, revised it, obtained all the required signatures, and filed it with your university. You might have even purchased a new pair of shoes to wear under your gown for commencement. You have officially completed all the requirements for your degree, but your adviser may be hinting that you are not finished. If so, your adviser is probably referring to scholarly publication of all or a part of your thesis/dissertation.

PUBLISHING SCHOLARLY ARTICLES

Technically, publishing scholarly articles from your thesis/dissertation research is not part of the degree requirement. People can and do graduate with their degrees without publication credits. But, if your planned career includes a position in academia, especially at a research-focused university, knowing how to publish academic papers would be a fantastic last skill to learn before leaving the university.

Your adviser as a collaborative writing partner

Because your research was done under the tutelage of your adviser and he or she will be helping you get it published, it is common courtesy to include him or her as an author on the academic paper. There is a lot that goes into the order of the names listed on a paper. So, until you understand all the customs and considerations, allow your adviser to decide the order. Do not risk jeopardizing one of the most important professional relationships you will ever develop over feelings of ownership or pride. You have your entire career to publish more papers and be listed as first author.

While preparing the paper, your adviser will probably still take the lead. But, you will be more or less equal partners in this publishing venture, so you will need to show initiative and the willingness to express preferences, along with the reasons for those preferences. Writing your thesis/dissertation technically was collaboration but one in which there were clear authoritative and subordinate roles. Revising a portion of your thesis/dissertation into an article will entail functioning together as co-authors with a codetermined division of labor. And, with the paper, you have the advantage of choice. You do not have to do it to earn your degree. Instead, you are choosing to go the extra mile, which can help emotionally if things get a little tense.

Adapting your thesis/dissertation

The typical scholarly article is more focused than a thesis/dissertation. With the latter document, you are expected to select a complex research problem that encompasses multiple facets. With the former document, one facet is normally all that is covered. This means it is the rare thesis/dissertation that is published in a journal in the same exact state as the version written for the graduate committee. Knowing how to parse the information in your thesis/dissertation takes a bit of experience and a lot of reading, which is why it is so beneficial to have your adviser walk you through this division of content the first time. The necessary revision steps will vary from discipline to discipline and target journal to target journal. But, the ultimate goal is the same: Pull out a meaningful piece of the whole, and publish it in a digestible format.

Submitting to peer-reviewed journals

After all the reading you have done in your research, you probably have a good feel for which journals your research would best fit. Your adviser will also be able to give you guidance once the content of your article is agreed upon. Each journal will have its own submission guidelines, so visit the journal's website and search for author instructions. Some journals, like some universities, now have an electronic submission system so you may have to create accounts before submitting your files. As with any other area of the publishing industry, competition is fierce. This is why you should take advantage of learning the publishing ropes with your adviser, especially if he or she has an established name or reputation in your field. Your adviser will also have a better feel for when the paper is ready to be submitted, thus saving you both the embarrassment of a less-than-professional piece of work.

If your work is accepted for publication, you will be able to list it on your resume as "forthcoming" while you look for new positions. Having a list of publications under your belt is a definite plus when looking for tenure-track positions in academia, as well as positions in research laboratories. If you just earned your master's degree and intend to go for your doctorate as well, having publications to your credit may also help you land a spot with a more prestigious adviser or university.

CASE STUDY: DON'T GET TOO CAUGHT UP

Scott E. Foss, Ph.D.
Regional Paleontologist, Bureau of
Land Management
scott_foss@blm.gov
www.ut.blm.gov

BIOGRAPHY:

After working with the National Park Service at both the Badlands National Park and John Day Fossil Beds National Monument, Dr. Foss now works for the Bureau of Land Management (BLM). He serves as a Paleontology Program Lead for the Utah BLM and a BLM Paleontology Technical Lead for Nevada, Oregon, and Washington. He also serves on the Interagency Coordination Team for the Paleontological Resources Preservation Act (PRPA). Dr. Foss is an expert in paleontology, public policy in conjunction with paleontology, and museum curation. With his advanced education in geological, anatomical, and biological sciences, he also serves as a Courtesy Assistant Professor in the Department of Geological Sciences at Oregon State University.

DISSERTATION TITLE AND SYNOPSIS:

Systematics and Paleobiology of the Entelodontidae (Mammalia, Artiodactyla)

This dissertation is essentially a review of the extinct family *Entelodontidae* with suggested taxonomic revisions and morphological (anatomical reconstructions and functional interpretations) and paleoecological (behavior, diet, and life history) interpretations.

FIRST-PERSON ACCOUNT:

Results from my dissertation have appeared in many of my subsequent publications, most notably the book *The Evolution of the Artiodactyls.* I have also presented portions of the results of my dissertation at multiple professional meetings, starting with the Society of Vertebrate Paleontology, and most recently in a talk delivered to the Geological Society of America.

I have also delivered multiple lectures on entelodonts as an invited speaker at the University of Oregon, Oregon State University, Pacific Lutheran University, the University of Utah, Utah Friends of Paleontology, and Paleofest. I have worked as a technical adviser for entelodont anatomical and ecological reconstruction for *National Geographic*, *Discovery*, the BBC, Creative Differences Studios, and Hive Studios. I have also discussed entelodont behavior and ecology for the above production companies and multiple news media outlets. All of this is a direct outgrowth of my dissertation research.

I have worked with many production companies over the years. The BBC's *Walking with Prehistoric Beasts* (WWPB) filmed in 2000 and was released in 2001. I worked as a technical adviser for approximately two years. Prior to that, I had worked with public television and news media outlets, but at the time, this was the largest production with which I had been involved. Since then, I have worked with equally large productions for *National Geographic* and the *Discovery Channel*.

In the case of WWPB, I was chosen because the producers wanted to reconstruct an entelodont, and I was the only person currently working on the family *Enteolodontidae*. At the time, I had not yet defended my dissertation, but my work was well known to my colleagues, who recommended me to the producers of the show.

The experience was complex in that it was both thrilling to see interpretations from my dissertation accurately scripted and portrayed but frustrating to see the anatomical reconstructions so dramatically altered from my descriptions. Travel to museum and field locations in order to film spots is always an outstanding experience that requires long days, stamina, and rigorous professionalism. One frustration is that ratings are often more important than accuracy, and producers want to see prehistoric beasts fight. Although entelodonts most certainly did fight, it would be nice to see a more balanced portrayal of a day in the life of one of these beasts. Overall, the BBC was very good to work with.

I have two tips for graduate students about how to write a successful thesis/dissertation. First, although thesis or dissertation writing is worthy of taking seriously and doing well, do not give it any more importance than any other step in your career. It is a milestone, but there will be more milestones in your career, so get it behind you and move on to the next one. I think people who put too much importance on their theses/dissertations get hung up and often do not finish.

For my graduate experience, I envisioned writing the ultimate monograph on the group. I have continued to pursue the same research questions I was asking as a graduate student, and I'm still not ready to write that monograph. After exceeding my schedule by two years with no end in sight, I decided to write a summary of everything I knew about my topic. I did all I could to impress my committee by overwhelming them with all of the information I had collected. However, they were not impressed, and I failed my first defense. Two of my committee members were outright hostile to me about the length of the work. One committee member suggested that it read like I was bragging. I went back and rewrote my dissertation. The rewritten version came in at 222 pages (shorter than many master's theses in my discipline) compared to my original, which was nearly 800 pages.

This leads to my second piece of advice. Brevity and clarity are far more important than length. Great chefs know how to use the best ingredients, combine them in the right way, and then boil them down to a paradoxically complex yet subtle sauce. Great writing should be the same.

PRESENTING AT PROFESSIONAL MEETINGS

If publishing your research in a scholarly article is not working out, or even if it is, you may want to consider presenting your research at professional meetings. Conferences, normally put on by professional organizations, are a great way to practice your networking and communication skills; plus, they can also get you noticed in a larger academic community. You may even meet your future employer there or hear about a post-doctoral fellowship you would like to pursue. The types of research-sharing opportunities you have at these professional meetings are:

- Workshops/seminars, in which you stand before an audience, present a portion of your research, and field inquiry and challenge-style questions — somewhat like your defense.

- White papers, which are short technical papers written in academic language presented in a more conversational manner, accompanied by a slideshow and followed with inquiry-style questions from the audience.

- Poster sessions, in which you mount visuals and short descriptions of your research on boards such as foam-core boards or rigid poster board. These boards are hung on display throughout a conference, but you only stand by the board at specified times to field questions. Consider your poster to be a visual advertisement of your research.

SOCIALIZING AND NETWORKING

With the advent of online directories of professionals and social media, connecting with other people who share your research interest is easier than ever. You are no longer limited to meeting people at conference mixers over a glass of flat champagne. Taking part in a vibrant and well-moderated online community will not only facilitate your inclusion in discussions that include your topics of interest, but it will also get you noticed by the press, as they search these communities for potential interviewees. Production companies for documentaries search online for experts and peer reviewers as well — a potentially excellent credit to add to your resume. Ask around campus for suggestions, or do an online search of "[your research topic] + [leading author] + [network]" and see what comes up. You will be able to tell pretty quickly which networks are good or not by the number of ads on the site and the frequency with which people sign in and participate.

If you have limited time to network, start by joining well-known professional organizations in your discipline and creating an account to access their online features. This way, you will be able to update your profile so other members (and potentially the media) can find you. Register your information with your university's alumni group. Although it may mean being asked for donations from time to time, your alumni group will be the most interested in broadcasting your professional successes in the future. Lastly, stay in touch with your adviser, if at all possible. He or she has invested a lot of time and energy in you and your work. If you strive to repay it by diligently seeking employment and using the skills he or she taught you, connections and tips may fall your way at just the right moment.

Appendix A

SAMPLE NOTE-TAKING FORM

Authors: Source #:

Article/Chapter Title: Keywords:

Journal/Book Title:

Storage Location:

Publisher: City: Year:

Official statement of the Research Problem:

Major Results   Page(s)

1.

2.

3.

Major Conclusions   Page(s)

1.

2.

3.

Other Key Points that Apply to My Research Problem   Page(s)

Their Point   *My Reaction*

1.

2.

Quotations   Page(s)

1.

2.

3.

Notable Items from the Writing Style:

Notable Items from the Methodology: Page(s)

1. Research Type:

2. Data Collection:

3. Data Analysis:

4. Rationale for the Researchers' Choices:

Appendix B

LIST OF ORGANIZATIONAL RESOURCES

CNET

Online review site

www.cnet.com

- Professional and customer reviews of many electronic devices

- Good for selecting scanners, external hard-drives, and laptop computers

- Free access

Dropbox

Online Web application

www.dropbox.com

- Free synchronization utility for files

- Installed software on your computer provides automated synchronization

- Browser-based utility provides access to files from any computer

- Smartphone application available

Evernote

Online Web application

www.evernote.com

- Free and premium services

- Installed software on your computer provides swift document capture, tagging, and synchronization

- Browser-based utility provides access to files from any computer

- Synchronization with Nozbe™ available

- Smartphone application available

Getting Things Done: The Art of Stress-Free Productivity
By: David Allen
Book; Available in paperback and e-book from booksellers

- Guidance on setting up an organizational system

- Proposal for a new way of thinking about projects, tasks, and deadlines

- Strategies for maximizing productivity in professional and personal arenas

- Tips for paper and electronic systems

Get Organized®
Online shop
www.shopgetorganized.com/home_office/201306

- Compact workspace solutions

- Mobile filing solutions

- Paper management systems more unique than those at an office supply store

Nozbe
Online Web application
www.nozbe.com

- Free and premium services

- Task tracking for projects

- Alignment with David Allen's *Getting Things Done* organizational method

- Synchronization with Evernote available

- Smartphone application available

Zotero
Web browser plug-in
www.zotero.org

- Free management tool for research sources, collaboration, and projects

- Requires Firefox Web browser

- Some special interest forums available for tips that apply to specific disciplines

Appendix C

LIST OF ADDITIONAL WRITING RESOURCES

Dissertation and Thesis Paper Samples
Blog
http://thesissamples.blogspot.com

- Samples of the various chapters from random works

- Good for a beginning look but no guarantee as to the success or failure of these samples

Dissertation Handout from University of North Carolina at Chapel Hill
Web page
www.unc.edu/depts/wcweb/handouts/dissertation.html

- Strategies for avoiding "ABD" (all but degree)

- Tips for organizing time, content, and momentum

- Discussion of stress factors and associated coping strategies

Learner Associates

Website

http://learnerassociates.net

- Provides free access to books about the thesis/dissertation journey

- Includes the full text for the book *Writing and Presenting Your Thesis or Dissertation* by S. Joseph Levine

- Discussion of the concepts presented in these materials is available on Facebook at **www.facebook.com/pages/Writing-and-Presenting-Your-Thesis-or-Dissertation/112349848788439**

Making a Thesis or Dissertation Support Group Work for You

PDF document

www.rackham.umich.edu/downloads/publications/DissSuppGrp.pdf

- Strategies for joining and utilizing writing support group services

- Tips on what to avoid in support groups

Online Writing Lab at Purdue (OWL)

Website

http://owl.english.purdue.edu

- Tutorials on grammar, organization of content, and research

- Style guides

- Strategies for English as a Second Language (ESL)

Piled Higher and Deeper (Ph.D. Comics)

Website

www.phdcomics.com

- Stress relief via laughs

- Showcase of pitfalls to avoid

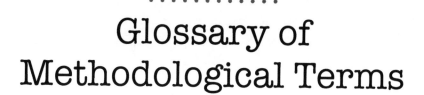

Glossary of Methodological Terms

Abstract: A one-page summary that presents a research problem along with the methodology and major findings of the associated research study.

Academic journal: A peer-reviewed publication that serves as the core means of disseminating the latest findings from research within a particular topic or discipline.

Analysis: The process of taking a mass of individual facts and boiling them down into one or more statements that contribute to a discipline.

Annual review: A book-length survey of the latest research topics within a given discipline.

Appendices: Short batches of information grouped together at the end of a thesis/dissertation that shed light on the major text.

Applied research: Research conducted for the sake of discovering or improving something.

Basic research: Research conducted for the sake of knowing something.

Causal-comparative: A research design that searches for the causation of phenomena after they have occurred.

Central tendency: A statistical method that generates an average value for a particular variable, which allows a pool of data to be represented by a single number.

Conclusions: Thoughts and opinions about the research problem that are informed by the background, methodology, and results of the research project. *See "summary" for the information that usually accompanies the conclusions in the last section of a thesis/dissertation.*

Content analysis: A method of asking a question and then searching existing literature and sources for information that suggests an answer to that question.

Correlation: A statistical method that quantifies the likelihood that two variables are related.

Correlational: A research design that searches for relationships between factors.

Data: Information collected and analyzed in exploration of a research problem.

Data manipulation: Selective analysis of data to increase the likelihood that the outcome will support the researcher's predictions.

Descriptive: A research design that gathers information about a topic for which little is known, calculating averages, percentages, and frequencies.

Experimental: A research design that uses control groups, well-defined manipulation of the other groups, and random assignment of subjects into these groups.

Extrinsic benefit: An external reward or benefit a person earns by doing a task.

Heuristics: Generalized guidelines in a discipline that suggest which sample size to use based on the data-collection method and the size of the pool being sampled.

Hypothesis: A research problem written as a statement of prediction as to the effect a given factor will have on a situation or trait.

Incomplete data set: A group of results missing information about a particular factor or subject.

Interview: A data-collection method that records verbal responses of a study subject to a researcher's questions.

Intrinsic benefit: A positive internal thing that a person gains by doing a task.

Literature: The entire body of knowledge within a given discipline.

Literature review: A section of a thesis/dissertation that familiarizes a reader with pertinent sources of information used to conceptualize, design, conduct, and analyze a particular research project.

Methodology: The description of how a person will do (or did) a research problem, including descriptions of research subjects, locations, data collection procedures, and analysis procedures.

Monograph: A detailed treatment of a specific area of a given discipline.

Multivariate analysis: A statistical method that looks for variance or correlation between multiple variables and predicts whether the results are applicable beyond the study groups.

Null hypothesis: A statement that predicts there will be no effect of a given factor on the variable in question.

Observation: The process by which a researcher watches a study subject and records information about what that subject is doing or saying.

Outliers: Data points on the extreme edges of a data range.

Poster session: A segment of a professional meeting in which a person displays a short description of a research project, mounted on stiff board, and fields informal questions.

Power analysis: A method for calculating sample size based on how large or small a difference the analysis must detect.

Practical research: *See "applied research."*

Pure research: *See "basic research."*

Quasi-experimental: A research design similar to experimental design yet does not use random assignment of subjects into study groups.

Question: A research problem that asks what effect a factor will have on a given situation or trait.

Questionnaire: Written responses of study subjects to pre-defined questions.

Repeated measures: A data-collection method that quantifies the state of a variable in a study subject across regular time intervals.

Representative sample: The number of subjects and their overall characteristics that will allow a researcher to generalize the findings to the entire pool from which the sample was drawn.

Research problem: The particular question or hypothesis that is the basis of a thesis/dissertation.

Results: Data (information) gathered according to a pre-determined methodology in order to explore a research problem.

Seminar: A meeting in which a person presents research to an audience and fields inquiry and challenge-style questions.

Significance: A statistical test that predicts the likelihood that differences found in descriptive statistics are true differences.

Source: A journal article, lecture, interview, or other piece of media used to provide information regarding a particular research problem.

Summary: A brief overview of the background, methodology, and results of a research project. *See "conclusions" for the information that usually accompanies the summary in the last section of a thesis/dissertation.*

Test: A data-collection method that measures the performance of pre-defined variables in response to pre-defined factors.

Variance: A statistical method that quantifies the amount of difference individual data points have from the mean of those points.

White paper: A short technical paper written in academic language that is presented in front of an audience in conversational manner and followed with inquiry-style questions.

Workshop: *See "seminar."*

Bibliography

"Adjunct," *Merriam-Webster Dictionary Online*. May 11, 2010. **www. merriam-webster.com/dictionary/adjunct**.

"ANOVA/MANOVA," *StatSoft Electronic Statistics Textbook*. May 11, 2010. **www.statsoft.com/textbook/anova-manova**.

Archambault, Susan, *"Pearson R."* Wellesley College. May 11, 2010. **www.wellesley.edu/Psychology/Psych205/pearson.html**.

Clark, Irene L., *Writing the Successful Thesis and Dissertation: Entering the Conversation*, Prentice Hall, Upper Saddle River, 2007.

"Definition of: Boolean Logic," *PCMAG.COM Encyclopedia*. May 11, 2010. **www.pcmag.com/encyclopedia_term/0,2542,t=Boolean+log ic&i=38836,00.asp**.

"Digest of Education Statistics: 2008," National Center for Education Statistics. April 1, 2010. **http://nces.ed.gov/programs/digest/d08**.

"Document Camera," Facilities Management: The University of Iowa. May 10, 2010. **http://classrooms.uiowa.edu/multimediaforms/ DocumentCamera.pdf**.

Garner, Bryan A., *"Grammar and Usage:" The Chicago Manual of Style [CD-ROM], 15th edition*, The University of Chicago Press, Chicago, 2003.

Gauvin, Marty, *"Riding the Cloud with Third Generation Outsourcing,"* Cloud Computing Expo. April 8, 2010. **http:// cloudcomputingexpo.com/node/1346512/print**.

Glatthorn, Allan A. and Randy L. Joyner, *Writing the Winning Thesis or Dissertation: A Step-by-Step Guide, 2nd edition*, Corwin Press, Thousand Oaks, 2005.

"Hypothesis," Merriam-Webster Dictionary Online. April 29, 2010. **www. merriam-webster.com/dictionary/hypothesis**.

Kastens, Kim et al., *"How to Write Your Thesis,"* Columbia University: Earth Institute. June 24, 2010. **www.ldeo.columbia.edu/~martins/ sen_sem/thesis_org.html**.

Key, James P., *"Module S7 - Chi Square,"* Research Design in Occupational Education. May 11, 2010. **www.okstate.edu/ag/ agedcm4h/academic/aged5980a/5980/newpage28.htm**.

"Know Your Money: How to Detect Counterfeit Currency," United States Secret Service. April 11, 2010. **www.secretservice.gov/money_ detect.shtml**.

Levine, S. Joseph, *Writing and Presenting Your Thesis or Dissertation* [e-book], Learner Associates, East Lansing, 2005.

Lunenburg, Fred C. and Beverly J. Irby, *Writing a Successful Thesis or Dissertation: Tips and Strategies for Students in the Social and Behavioral Sciences*, Corwin Press, Thousand Oaks, 2008.

Ogden, Evelyn Hunt, *Complete Your Dissertation or Thesis in Two Semesters or Less*, Rowman & Littlefield Publishers, Inc., Lanham, 2007.

Peterson, Don, *"Bibliographies: Tutorials for OpenOffice."* June 29, 2010. **www.tutorialsforopenoffice.org/tutorial/Bibliographies.html**.

Thomas, R. Murray and Dale L. Brubaker, *Theses and Dissertations: A Guide to Planning, Research, and Writing*, Bergin & Garvey, Westport, 2000.

Turabian, Kate L., *A Manual for Writers of Research Papers, Theses, and Dissertations: Chicago Style for Students and Researchers, 7th edition*, The University of Chicago Press, Chicago, 2007.

Webster's New World College Dictionary [Mobile v1.5], 4th edition, Wiley Publishing, Inc., Cleveland, 2002.

Author Biography:

J.S. Graustein earned a master's in Ecology from Northern Illinois University and then taught college-level Biology for two years at College of Notre Dame in Belmont, California. She switched her focus to writing after starting a family. She now writes poetry, nonfiction, and flash fiction for children and adults. Her work has appeared in print and online publications. She inherited Folded Word, a small indie press, from Founding Editor Jessie Carty in April 2009. Since then, J.S. has edited and produced Folded Word's first chapbooks and books. She also serves as Submissions Chair for Surprise Valley Writers Conference in Cedarville, California.

Index